A long-awaited-for practical resource that every missions leader must have and should use! This book's impressiveness lies in how it has been founded not only on sound theological and missiological convictions, but on transparent conversations amongst leaders with first-hand long term cross-cultural experiences, who are committed to making church-missions agency partnerships work. The book's intentional challenge for missions leaders to build on and add to this body of much needed literature, with practical handles on how to do so, gives much hope for effective kingdom partnerships in missions. Every missions leader should take this book seriously!

Christy Lim, Singapore Director, InterServe

You are holding the product of years of prayer, research and practical partnership by the people in the CMAT team. It is special on two counts – it is birthed not through theory and study but through tested experience, and it is a project initiated and led by an Asian pastor. It is timely because it is published when the global church and missions community are grappling with issues associated with the rise of the church in the global south, the comparative weakening of the western church, the rise of "direct-sending", "short-term" and "self-sending" missions, and the myriad challenges of effective and sustainable partnership between local churches and missions agencies.

Daniel Wong, National Director, OMF Singapore

Ivan Liew has given us a timely book on mission partnerships. Those who see "Mission" as God's redemptive work will be challenged to use the materials as invaluable resources to formulate meaningful and enduring partnership with churches, agencies and individuals. Though the book is set primarily in a Singapore context, the fundamental principles make it applicable to other contexts. I recommend this book wholeheartedly.

Dianna Khoo, Country Director
Methodist Missions Society, Singapore

The modern context of missions in Singapore necessitates that churches and mission agencies work together in partnership for greater effectiveness and impact. Good partnership reflects the Trinitarian nature of God and the unity we have in Christ and is crucial for our overall witness in missions. This book gives an excellent foundation and basis for a conversation to start between churches and mission agencies.

David Tan, Executive Director, Wycliffe Singapore

This book is absolutely critical for all our missions-sending churches. It is well researched, and gives practical and realistic perspectives of what is needed for churches and mission agencies in collaborating and partnering to fulfil Christ's Great Commission.

Jim Chew, Missions Mentor, The Navigators

Churches and Missions Agencies Together stands out among many books on missions partnership issues. Written within the Singaporean church-agency context, the issues dealt with and the solutions advanced apply globally. The timely insights cross national, ethnic and linguistic barriers; they are invaluable lessons for mission agencies and churches alike around the world. Indeed, if churches and missions agencies take the lessons to heart and apply the recommendations, we would see stronger partnerships become the norm, and more workers raised up for God's harvest as churches and mission agencies build better synergy. This is a must-read for missions and church leaders, missionaries and church members alike. I highly recommend it.

Joshua Bogunjoko, International Director, SIM International

The Local Church and the Mobile Church both have their place in the Kingdom of God. Together we can accomplish much in fulfilling the Great Commission-reaching the Last, the Least and the Lost. *Churches and Missions Agencies Together,* if put into practice, will bring us a step forward to fulfilling Jesus' longing: "May they be brought to complete unity to let the world know that you sent me and have loved them even as you have loved me."

Joseph Chean, Director, YWAM Singapore

In our age of globalisation, the Church needs to actively engage with global issues in world evangelisation. Thank God we can leverage on our interconnectedness as the global body of Christ for we cannot do this alone. *Churches and Missions Agencies*

Together exemplifies such partnership in missions that is needed to effectively minister the gospel. May the world witness the love of Christian disciples as we learn to serve with one another in and through missions.

Lawrence Ko, National Director
Singapore Centre for Global Missions

A highly commendable book with insightful analysis of church and missions agency partnership from the historical, theological and practical perspectives. The rich spectrum of case studies from the Singapore context brings to light the importance of partnership values, particularly the biblical centrality of the church, glad submission and mutual deference. A very resourceful handbook for pastors, missions leaders and church missions committees.

Patrick Fung, General Director, OMF International

Given the lack of publications and local research in this important area, *Churches and Missions Agencies Together* makes a valuable contribution that "stands in the gap." Although the focus is on medium-sized Singapore churches, this book is a must-read for all Christian leaders with a heart for people around the world who are living and dying without hearing of Jesus. By working together, smaller churches could also benefit from the many helpful conclusions and recommendations herein. It is also a wake-up call to those taking the less costly path of direct-send and short-term missions. I especially commend this book to leaders of churches and missions agencies.

Philip Marshall, Missiologist, SIM International

This book is a breakthrough in cooperation between churches and missions agencies, guiding our manoeuvres amidst the ambiguity of the tripartite relationship in missionary sending. It provides an essential blueprint for successful partnerships. Every church, agency and missionary should have a copy!

Stanley Ling, Regional Director, SIM East Asia

An easy-to-digest book that clearly contributes to missiology literature that is relevant to the Singapore context. The question is not whether you should read this, for you should, but how you can put these concepts of partnership into intentional action for God's kingdom!

Willy Ong, Executive Director, OM Singapore

ENDORSED BY CHURCHES

Churches and Missions Agencies Together is both timely and rich in information on better practices and pitfalls to avoid in church-agency partnerships. It will serve as an invaluable resource as churches seek to continue partnering with missions agencies, and as they review and refine missions policies in the future. Thanks be to God for guiding the team in laying the foundation and building up this body of knowledge!

Colin Liaw, Missions Chairman, Praise EFC, Singapore

Kudos to the authors for helping us think through the pros and cons of churches working either with or independent of missions agencies. The case studies are particularly helpful in highlighting common problems to which every church and missions agency should be prepared to respond.

Gordon Wong, President, Trinity Annual Conference
Methodist Church of Singapore

Ivan Liew has promoted gospel work in some of the most challenging cross-cultural situations in the world as a missions pastor for over ten years. To his credit, he never worked alone but partnered agencies and other churches. The book's content is not shallow, comprising valuable theological emphasis on the relevance of the Holy Trinity and frank discussion on how things can turn out in the missions field between churches, agencies and missionaries. All interested in promoting Christian missions should read this book and learn from the experiences and insights contained herein.

Malcolm Tan, Pastor-in-Charge
Covenant Community Methodist Church, Singapore

This book is must-have companion for anyone new to the missions ministry and an essential for anyone who has been involved in missions work. It provides a deep grasp of the issues involving all key stakeholders in missions work and ways to effectively manage them based upon Trinitarian values and principles. The model provides a robust foundation for an effective missions programme, reflecting different perspectives of partners.

Ooi Chee Kong, Missions Deacon
Family of Grace Evangelical Free Church, Singapore

Churches and Missions Agencies Together provides a healthy and constructive framework for ministry together. It guides us into a much-needed complementary ministry relationship that is rarely emphasised. The pulse of the Singaporean church is captured through research and experience. The ingredients for an effective partnership will guide anyone wanting to build ministry over the long term. As a life-long missions practitioner in the local church, I highly recommend this book.

Steve Beirn, **Pastor of Global Ministries, Calvary Church**
Lancaster, Pennsylvania, USA

A good resource on "how-to" and best practices of churches and missions agencies…

Terence Goh, **Pastoral Team Staff**
Barker Road Methodist Church, Singapore

This book is a rare gem for those keen on the implementation of missions. Key trends, roles of para-church organisations, and greater recent ownership of local churches in the Great Commission form the basis of a tripartite relational model for church-agency partnership. The writing is well researched with consultation and input from experienced practitioners. I highly recommend *Churches and Missions Agencies Together* to denominational heads, senior pastors, mission pastors, missions committee members and chairpersons.

Wong Foo Mun, **English Presbytery Missions Committee Chairman**
Presbyterian Church of Singapore

Churches and Missions Agencies Together serves as an excellent resource for churches and mission agencies that want to learn more about how to deal with each other as true brothers and sisters in Christ while advancing the gospel. The book deals with the very practical questions of sharing resources and responsibilities.

Yeap Eng Hooi, **Missions Chairman**
All Saints Presbyterian Church Singapore

This book models what fruitful church-agency partnerships can look like, with honest dialogue and nuanced reflection informing practical steps forward. Whether your church is just starting to catch a vision for what God is doing in the world, or thinking through how to more effectively send and support long-term cross-cultural workers, we would encourage you to read and consider what is modelled here.

Ailene & Benjamin Grandey, Coordinators
Perspectives Course Singapore

Wouldn't churches and missions agencies together be nice? They could share their strengths, create synergistic partnerships without envy and celebrate sowing seeds in God's harvest. Instead, I have heard hundreds of stories around the world where this partnership is challenging, full of conflict and not working. The real victims are often the missionaries... The book you hold in your hands is a gold mine. It not only looks at solid research data and theological discussions, but also goes a step further to look at the practice of ministry and implementation points in the context of the sending nation of Singapore. Indeed, it is a gold mine of learning and inspiration toward reflective dialogue for all sending nations, sending churches and sending missions agencies today.

Harry Hoffmann, Global Member Care Network Coordinator
WEA Mission Commission

This book portrays a delightful facet of the global missions enterprise. Church and mission leaders from South East Asia present a model that can benefit the worldwide church in strengthening member care for those who are working cross-culturally. The policies and best practices developed here are based on a strong theological framework, peer-reviewed research and case studies. These were developed by a working group that modelled honest discussion and collaboration between church and missions leaders. Working groups in many places can take note of this model and join in the process of strengthening member care globally. May God use this book to impact his kingdom worldwide!

Jim Pluedemann, Professor of Intercultural Studies
Trinity Evangelical Divinity School, USA

As I read this book, I had two thoughts. First, "I wish I had written that!" and second, "I wish my church and our pastors would read this!" I read with appreciation and took copious notes because I sense that this material could be very useful to me in our current church situation, especially with regard to its approach to missions. It is useful for me now, and will be also to every missionary, mission agency, church missions committee, pastor whose church has any involvement in missions, and every member care practitioner and thinker. It is exceedingly well written and very clear, progressing well from theory and research to practical aspects and applications. The final challenge, "Start your own CMAT" brings the necessary response home to the reader immediately.

Laura Mae Gardner

Author of *Healthy, Resilient and Effective in Cross-Cultural Ministry*

Churches and Missions Agencies Together brings together the rich practical experiences and knowledge of various missions stakeholders that will help provide greater insights to those involved in church-agency partnerships and the provision of member care. This is a vital real-life handbook for anyone with an interest in missions mobilisation.

Philip Chang, **Regional Director for South East Asia**

Lausanne Movement

Each time I visit Singapore, I am challenged and encouraged by the passion, commitment and thinking of the churches and agencies engaged in global missions. This book is evidence of that and their commitment to partnership in our gospel endeavour. I pray that this book will strengthen the church-agency partnership movement further and be used by others to learn these important lessons.

Rob Hay, **Principal, Redcliffe College, UK**

The potential for kingdom collaboration between churches and missions agencies is as ancient as the Church of Antioch and Paul's Missionary Band in the Book of Acts. Yet, sadly, many churches fail to understand that the agency is needed to extend the worldwide mission of the church. In *Churches and Mission Agencies Together*, Ivan Liew provides a practical, case study guide that gives us effective patterns for how this collaboration can happen. I commend this volume to churches and missions agencies alike. The modality of the church and the sodality of the agency need each other if we are to reach the world for Jesus Christ!

Timothy Tennent, President and Professor of World Christianity

Asbury Theological Seminary, USA

Ivan Liew offers a well-reasoned and theologically rich model for church-mission agency relationships. He calls practitioners to journey from arms-length transactions to full relational embrace of the missionary as the congregation and agency own their unique contributions in a spirit of mutuality. More than describing what ought to be, the book stands on sound research of best practices. The "family at home" (church) and the 'family at work" (agency) embody the Spirited dance of Trinitarian love and respect on behalf of the one(s) sent to the field. This text will equip local missions committees, and the agency staff who work with them, to holistically care for the Gospel-bearers. For the sake of God's mission, live this book!

Thomas Tumblin, Professor of Leadership

Asbury Theological Seminary, USA

CHURCHES & MISSIONS AGENCIES
TOGETHER

a relational model for partnership practice

CHURCHES & MISSIONS AGENCIES
TOGETHER

a relational model for partnership practice

edited by
IVAN LIEW

ISBN: 979-8-42-503103-7

Book cover and interior layout by Sarah O'Neal | eve custom artwork

Front cover image was created with several images courtesy of iStockphoto/sorendls, iStockphoto/WichitS, and Shutterstock/BonAppetit. The back cover was created using a photo courtesy of Alamy Stock Photo/JSCallahan/tropicalpix

To order this book, please visit:
Amazon.com

CONTRIBUTORS

Belinda Ng is SIM East Asia's Member Care & MK Consultant, part of the Pastoral Care Team, and an executive committee member of the Global Member Care Network. She served as a missionary with SIM for 12 years in Niger, then as a personnel director for 16 years, sending Asian missionaries through numerous church partnerships.

Dr Brent Lindquist is the President of Link Care Center, in Fresno California, USA. Link Care is a counselling and pastoral care center for missionaries and pastors in US denominations and mission organizations. He also consults for mission groups as part of Missio Nexus, and is a learning architect for Crosswired, a global online learning and collaborative community.

Daphne Teo is a member of the OMF Singapore Home Council and chairs the Member Care subcommittee. She also sits on the Board of Sponsors and Management Board of Singapore Bible College. Daphne holds an MA in pastoral counselling from Singapore Bible College.

Dr Jeffrey Lum is the Missions Director of Bartley Christian Church and a medical doctor who served in Cambodia with OMF Singapore from 2003 to 2013. He was seconded to Prison Fellowship Cambodia as their Medical Advisor and served as the Field Medical Advisor for the OMF Cambodia Field. He holds an MA in Intercultural Studies from Singapore Bible College.

Dr Kelvin Chen is the Deputy Regional Director for SIM East Asia. He previously served as a medical missionary in Nigeria with SIM and led an HIV/AIDS project that is still making an impact in the middle belt of Nigeria. He holds a medical degree from the National University of Singapore, a Master of Health Services Management from Curtin University, and an MDiv from Singapore Bible College.

Rev Leonard Leow is the SIM Singapore Director who actively partners churches in their missions endeavours and mentors potential cross-cultural workers. He previously served for 2 years with OM in Pakistan and 6 years as the Missions Pastor of Woodlands Evangelical Free Church. He holds an MA(Th) from the Melbourne School of Theology.

Ler Wee Meng serves as a deacon and missions committee member of Adam Road Presbyterian Church, sits on the English Presbytery Missions Committee, and is the Vice-Chairman of the New Tribes Mission Singapore board. He is the Managing Director of Securevision Pte Ltd, a security systems integrator and provider.

Lim Luck Yong is the Missions Pastor of Adam Road Presbyterian Church. He serves with the missions committee to send and care for the church's missionaries in multiple countries and coordinates the church's overseas missions efforts in the region.

Paul Tan is the Personnel and Candidature Manager in OMF Singapore. He previously served as a missionary in Thailand with OMF for 15 years in the literature and translation ministry and discipleship of believers, until he returned to Singapore in 2005.

Serene Lum is a missions staff at Bartley Christian Church, mobilizing the church and providing member care for missions personnel. She previously served on the mission field with OMF Cambodia from 2003 to 2013, supporting and helping new members and short-term missionaries adapt to ministry life on the field.

Thomas Lim is the missions pastor at Agape Baptist Church and a board member of International China Concern. He leads his church's ministry in Timor-Leste, where they partner a Brazilian missions agency to run a missions school.

Dr W M Syn is the Director of Pioneers in Asia. He previously served for 10 years as a missionary in India, focusing on community development, business as mission, and church planting strategies. He completed his DMiss at Biola University on the nature of partnership between the local church and missions agencies in Singapore.

CONTENTS

ACKNOWLEDGEMENTS

Ivan Liew

Though my name is on the front cover of this book, almost half of it was written by contributors and experienced practitioners who were instrumental for *Churches and Missions Agencies Together* springing to life. In the core steering committee, Belinda Ng, Daphne Teo and Jeffrey Lum played crucial roles in the formation and leadership of this group. Brent Lindquist was more than a consultant, affirming and guiding us (especially me) from the first day until now. All other members were far more than just contributors, for we grew in trust and friendship through the robust discussions that framed this entire book. Thanks to Daniel Wong, Kelvin Chen, Leonard Leow, Ler Wee Meng, Lim Luck Yong, Paul Tan, Serene Lum and Thomas Lim for this memorable two-year journey.

Our organisations have supported us in multiple ways, so we also want to thank the leadership of Adam Road Presbyterian Church, Agape Baptist Church, SIM East Asia, OMF Singapore and Pioneers inAsia, who backed our involvement in this project. In particular, Bartley Christian Church and Woodlands Evangelical Free Church not only encouraged their staff, but also jointly funded the ministry that led to the publication of this book.

I have pastored at Woodlands Evangelical Free Church for twelve years, and have been a part of this family for two decades. This community of faith has taught me about missions practice and the all-important role of relationships in church-agency partnership. The missions leaders before me had forged healthy partnerships with agencies, allowing me to research and uncover the gems they left in their path. Our missionaries have served sacrificially and shared their experiences transparently. This has made possible not just the telling of our partnership story, but also the discovery of our church-agency partnerships through research. To the elders, missions leadership and missionaries of Woodlands EFC, thank you for making all this possible.

The doctoral research behind this book was conducted at Asbury Theological Seminary, where I was abundantly blessed to be part of the Beeson International Leaders program. The academic and administrative staff of the Beeson International Center have equipped, inspired and encouraged me. My time with you was God's gift allowing me to write my dissertation on "Partnerships Between Local Churches and Missions Agencies" and dream of the completion of a book such as this. Thank you for planting and watering the seed.

To my wife, Renata, your prayer, respect and belief in me is an enabling encouragement every man desires. Thank you for being a wonderful life and ministry partner.

PREFACE
Brent Lindquist

Since the very first missions agency sent out its first missionary, local supporting churches and agencies have worked hard to figure out how best to care for their missionaries. Helping missionaries across organisational lines cope with cross-cultural ministry and work with multiple personalities is challenging, and it often is difficult to fully utilise the diverse gifts and desires of everyone involved. In a compact country like Singapore, difficulties are often well known and compounded in ways that are not apparent in other countries.

In 2014, a small group of missions agencies and church leaders came together to look for strategies to go beyond the status quo in member care. I was asked to join them as a consultant to the process, and as an aggregator for resources in the larger global sphere.

Initial meetings used a case-study approach describing the problems churches and missions agencies face, essentially with each other. This high degree of honesty and transparency resulted in a strong commitment to develop policies, white papers and other resources to be made available to the larger Singaporean church and missions community. This small group was never meant to be exclusive, but intended to serve as a transitory pilot group to develop ideas. It is hoped that, in the years to come, other working groups can join in the process to continue this development.

This resource presents a foundational model in two ways. First, the *Relational Model of Church-Agency Partnerships* provides a strong theological framework to undergird collaboration among missions agencies, churches and missionaries. Second, our pilot working group put these recommendations into practice, documented our progress and wrote this book. Thus, the contributors are themselves a relational model for future working groups.

We do not claim to be authoritative in all contexts or attempt to cover all church-agency partnership issues in this book. Instead, we reach out to others to add to a growing body of recommendations for good partnership practice.

Our major goal is to see churches and missions agencies come together in strong relationship, so that the missionaries they serve will sense deep commitment and care in all aspects of their missionary career. Of this, we are optimistic.

INTRODUCTION

Ivan Liew

The book you hold in your hand is the product of years of collaboration between several Singapore churches and the missions agencies through whom we send our missionaries. With great anticipation, we release this work, particularly to leaders of missions agencies and churches, in hopes that the contents will be a blessing to our ministries and the missionaries whom we send in our partnerships. The contents of this book are unique because they are not merely the opinions of one person from a church or an agency perspective. We present a foundational framework that arises out of peer-reviewed research and real-world practice from a group of church and missions agency leaders who have benefitted from the principles contained in these pages.

Part 1 of this book presents the background required to better grasp what constitutes partnership between a church and missions agency. First, the context of missions partnership is provided in Chapter 1, which is primarily written by W M Syn, the Singapore director of Pioneers inAsia. This chapter is part of his D.Miss. dissertation; therefore, further materials from him are available. Chapters 2–5 are written by Ivan Liew, the missions pastor of Woodlands Evangelical Free Church (Singapore), who formulated the thinking while working on his D.Min. dissertation on church-agency partnerships. Chapter 2 provides the biblical and theological bases, which are often lacking from discussions, for the role of the church and agency in their partnership. Drawing from Trinitarian theology, this chapter sets the foundation for values and models subsequently developed. Chapter 3 describes the research methods that formed the theoretical foundations on which this book is laid, and how the subsequent models were derived.

Chapters 4 and 5 take the theoretical models into the world of actual practice of partnerships between the church and missions agency, describing how a pilot working group of multiple agencies and churches was formed to apply this research and further develop it. This group calls itself "Churches and Missions Agencies Together (CMAT)", and this book is the result of our joint efforts. We present a model for missions leaders that describes the key ingredients that constitute a church-agency partnership, and provides guidelines for good practice based on biblical and theological foundations and values.

Part 2 of the book continues with practical discussions on these good practices. Each chapter in this section is jointly written by two to three members of CMAT, built around a case study discussed by the CMAT working group. The contents of each chapter represent good practice that is jointly agreed upon by CMAT members, and thus embody the consensus of multiple missions agency and church leaders. The good practice guidelines in Part 2 of the book are therefore distinctively powerful in that they are not only jointly proposed by a body of churches and agencies in active partnership with one another, but also based on peer-reviewed research validated by the feedback of missionaries sent in such partnerships. The following missions leaders in various churches and missions agencies contributed in this manner to the book. All are based in Singapore, except for our consultant Brent Lindquist, President of Link Care Center, Fresno California, USA.

CHURCHES	LEADERS
ADAM ROAD PRESBYTERIAN CHURCH	LER WEE MENG
	LIM LUCK YONG
AGAPE BAPTIST CHURCH	THOMAS LIM
BARTLEY CHRISTIAN CHURCH	JEFFREY LUM
	SERENE LUM
WOODLANDS EVANGELICAL FREE CHURCH	IVAN LIEW

MISSIONS AGENCIES	LEADERS
OMF SINGAPORE	DAPHNE TEO
	PAUL TAN
PIONEERS INASIA	W M SYN
SIM, SINGAPORE	BELINDA NG
	KELVIN CHEN
	LEONARD LEOW

CONSULTANT	
LINK CARE CENTER	BRENT LINDQUIST

Finally, Part 3 provides suggestions on how you can use the tools in this book to start your own CMAT group. This may be as simple as discussing the model with an existing partner and writing CMAT values into your own organisation's policies. If you are in partnership with multiple missions agencies or churches, you may wish to gather a small group and use the proven format that the pilot working group has developed. The original CMAT group will help you get started, further your discussions and build your own case studies. Such a group will not only improve your partnership practice tremendously, but also allow you to gain clarity and build relationships that will prove invaluable when challenges arise in the future.

After applying the models in this book, if your group is further interested in documenting your case studies and good practices with rigour, we welcome your collaboration for a future publication, which we could work on together in the spirit of missions partnership. In this manner, we seek to be catalysts for better partnerships between churches and missions agencies, for the glory of Christ among the nations.

DISCLAIMER

The stories and case studies contained in Part 2 and the annex of this book present names of fictitious missionaries, churches and missions agencies. All names in the original case studies have been changed from the actual scenarios. Some cases are a result of multiple situations blended together into a composite fictitious case. Gender, country, times and specific issues have all been significantly altered.

Therefore, any similarity to actual situation is purely coincidental, reflecting the fact that these are common foundational issues that many churches, missions agencies and missionaries repeatedly face in our partnerships.

CLARIFICATION

Woodlands Evangelical Free Church (Singapore) is the most frequently mentioned organisation in this book. It is an actual local church. The doctoral case-study research that first led to the *Relational Model of Church-Agency Partnerships (REMCAP)* arose from this local church.

Other organisations listed in Chapter 5 under "Participants of the CMAT Pilot Working Group" are also the actual names of churches, missions agencies and their leaders who contributed to the body of knowledge and authored this book.

part 1

A FRAMEWORK FOR CHURCH-AGENCY PARTNERSHIPS

chapter 1

CHURCHES & MISSIONS AGENCIES IN SINGAPORE

W M Syn

The world is not what it was twenty years ago, or even ten years ago. New enablers in the system are available to help global missions efforts: rapid air travel, information on the Internet, social media and access to relationships in an increasingly interconnected world. Although a wider range of strategies is available to the church, there are also greater limitations in increasingly closed nations. More and more, countries are monitoring missionary activity, and visas for long-term missionaries are being denied. In this increasingly complex environment, missions strategy needs to be more creative and the nature of what constitutes a "missionary" must be multidimensional.

The good news is we now have a plethora of choices in how we collectively resource global missions. On the other hand, many are walking away from traditional partnership approaches and many local churches are feeling they can sustain missions efforts on their own. Many are adopting the "direct-send" approach by sending their workers to the field without missions agency partnerships to support them. The relevance of missions agencies is being questioned and boundaries are being renegotiated. While some may feel that it is acceptable to work in our silos, in this chapter, I will contend that it is important that we work toward finding new common ground.

CHRISTIANITY IN SINGAPORE

Before we examine the evolving nature of missions partnership, it is worthwhile looking at the current state of missions in Singapore, especially since this book is drawn from a distinctly Singaporean context. This chapter draws from data gathered in a doctoral dissertation I undertook on the topic of partnership in missions. More than fifty stakeholders in the Singapore missions system were interviewed, and their voices have helped to paint a cohesive picture of the trends, strengths and weaknesses of this amazing movement that God is working to establish in South East Asia.

Factors Shaping Singaporean Churches and Missions Agencies

An online Economist Magazine article recently called Singapore "one of the world's great economic success stories."[1] This is not a unique use of such superlatives, and neither is such a title often questioned. The transformation of the small island nation since its independence in 1965 has taken it from being what some called, 'a small fishing village' to one of the major economic centres of the world. By almost any economic measure of growth, the postcolonial nation has led the way. Singapore's natural port and geographical location, which led it to be chosen by colonial Britain as a trading centre in South East Asia, has helped it to become a strategic centre for commerce, finance, networking and trade. It is also an entrepreneurial, travel and communications hub. Furthermore, it has the advantage of a large, English-speaking population, yet it is distinctly Asian. It is therefore seen as a cultural stepping stone between the East and West—very Asian, yet conveniently Western in many ways.

The Singaporean passport is one of the best in the world for visa-free travel, and the nation's entrepreneurial business-people are well networked in Asia and around the globe. The productive, efficient and success-oriented mindset behind the national economic miracle of Singapore also infuses missions in the city-state. The population has been shaped by the very success that the young nation has experienced since its independence in 1965, and this in turn infuses the way missions is done.

The tremendous numerical growth of the Singapore church was a precursor to its strong missions involvement. From an estimated 2% in 1970, the Christian population has grown to 18.3% in the 2010 census. Christianity has particularly flourished among the young, urbanised and English-educated Chinese (Goh 54). Likewise, missions involvement has been largely driven by English-speaking congregations, and some Singaporean leaders have also noted that there remains a greater opportunity to engage Chinese-speaking churches in missions.

The natural and spiritual success of the nation has become an added layer of missional conviction on the spirit of the church. Referring to the Great Commission, one church leader said, "Because of the phenomenal success of Singapore as a nation and because of Scripture, there is weight on our hearts which says [to us], 'to whom much is given, much is required'." The same leader went on to call it a "double conviction" on the nation in missions, a sense that the nation has been raised and called to be a blessing to other nations.

A Strategic Launching Point

One foreign-born church leader in Singapore commented on how globally minded the church in Singapore is, "I think location is a factor in the make-up of Singapore . . . It is kind of impossible to not be *global*. And if you are a Christian, *global* will always pull up the word, *missions*." The Singapore church, like the society, is urban, multicultural, cosmopolitan, multi-religious, multilingual, globally minded, well connected regionally, resource-rich and highly educated. Singapore is therefore seen as a strategic launching pad, resourcing centre and training hub for missions in the region.

Titles such as "the Antioch of Asia"—commonly attributed to either Rev Billy Graham or Rev Paul Yonggi Cho—have been pronounced on the nation. Opinions on the validity of the title vary; some have dismissed its value, while others have considered it a prophetic call on the nation. One church leader remarked that the Antioch call "is useful in that it focuses the energy in the churches," but others felt the church has yet to fully grasp what it truly means to be the Antioch of Asia. My feeling is that, when used in an appropriate manner, the title can be a rallying point and a benchmark or vision by which we can measure ourselves against and aspire to. However, if we use the title only as a badge of honour or an old report card, then we may slip into complacency or hubris.

History: Birthed by Missions

The history of the Singapore church also gives clues to the strength of its missions pedigree. A few short generations ago, it was itself a mission field where foreign missionaries planted young churches. Many of the church leaders who were involved in the interviews represented churches that were planted around the time of the nation's birth 50 years ago. These churches have recently celebrated their own 50th anniversary along with the nation. This heritage makes missions very much part of the DNA of the Singapore church and has driven many local churches to be involved in missions.

However, this growth of missions happened over many decades. One senior pastor reported that, during the early days of his ministry in the 1960s and 70s, there was, incredibly, little interest in missions. According to him, churches were more concerned with their own needs than meeting the needs of other nations. When he showed an interest in participating in some short-term missions trips, he was rebuked by his senior pastor with these words, "You should not do other people's work. You should do your own church's work."

In some ways, Singapore is the dream story of many modern missionaries, who are now looking forward to the day when their embryonic church plants will develop into self-supporting, self-governing and self-propagating churches. Within a few generations, we have seen the Singapore church grow from an exclusively missionary receiving church to a significant missionary sending one.

Good Missions Engagement by Churches

A healthy portion of the Singapore Church is aware of and motivated for missions, as attested to in my interviews with many leaders. Many churches have created the infrastructure to run with a missions vision: missions committee, missions policies, missions programmes, short-term missions teams and missions weeks in the church calendar. The implementation varies from church to church and denomination to denomination, but a number of leaders who work across Singapore independently concur in their estimations (from their anecdotal connections across the small nation) that at least a third of the churches are actively engaging in missions. They further estimated that another third of the churches have a desire to be engaged in missions and are growing in their ability to run with the vision, while the remaining third are yet to develop a missions vision and programme.

Many churches allocate large portions of their budget to missions (sometimes upwards of 20%, 30%, even 40% of their church budget), a sign of their capacity to give and their commitment to missions. A large portion of those interviewed support 100% of the financial needs of their long-term missionaries—something in Singapore that is almost unique in the world of missions. This practice of providing full support gives the local churches a strong sense of ownership of missions and the work. This in itself can be very healthy, but when accompanied with a paternalistic approach, it has also produced strategies that have come under criticism by indigenous partners and fellow missionaries.

The Nation Blessed by Church and Parachurch Organisations

The growth of the local churches has been a tremendous blessing to the nation, but interviewees also pointed out that parachurch organisations have also contributed significantly to the birth, growth and development of the church and missions endeavour. By the 1970s, many of the missions agencies have already been established in Singapore, and some had been present even before then.

Pastors and agency leaders go as far as to say that the strong presence of parachurches is one of the significant factors that helped in the growth of the church and enabled Singapore to become strong in missions. As one leader said, "I think the factor that many people may have ignored is the presence of missions agencies . . . Singapore churches are very privileged to be able to find speakers from any agencies, at any time. In other countries, they find it more difficult to find such resources to encourage them in missions." It is also said that many of the current generation of senior church leaders were themselves mentored, discipled and nurtured by parachurches.

FOUR COMMON MISSIONS APPROACHES

Churches in Singapore have many choices in the way they implement their missions vision. The following are the most common features of missions programmes. Although they are not unique to the global missions approach, they do represent the most common building blocks of Singaporean missions. There is also a unique mix of factors in Singapore that gives its missions programmes a distinctive flavour.

Long-Term Sending of Missionaries

Many churches in Singapore continue to send long-term missionaries. They do this in partnership with missions agencies that have well-established mobilisation processes, established member care practices, supportive field structures and experienced personnel. A growing "direct-send" approach. That is, they do it with minimal or no agency support. Some direct-send churches still utilise missions agency partnerships to help build their own capacity, rather than having an ongoing sending partnership.

Short-Term Teams

Short-term teams and programmes are global phenomena that continue to increase year after year, and such programmes are extensive in Singapore. Individual local churches have been known to send more than 50, 80 or 100 teams to the field in a year. It represents the primary way in which people can have first-hand experience on the field. They also help to provide programme support and missionary care. A good number of churches have six-month to one-year programmes, most often taken up by younger people prior to the start of their working career. Church leaders hope that these programmes will see an increasing number of people catching the vision for long-team service.

Most missions stakeholders agree that short-term trips can be extremely useful for mobilising, equipping and involving the body of Christ, as long as they are not seen as an end in themselves. The majority of the focus is on Asia, and Singapore's proximity allows teams to be sent in great numbers at a reasonable cost. The challenge of short-term approaches is ensuring that they are infused with cultural intelligence, and the best way to do this is to ensure that they are connected with a long-term strategy and relationship.

Non-Residential Approaches

Not only are numerous short-term teams sent out each year from Singapore churches, but many long-term ministry projects are often also undergirded by serial short-term visits, which sometimes act as a substitute for a long-term missionary presence. Another way of looking at serial short-term missions approaches is that they are non-residential approaches. Ex-missionaries utilise non-residential approaches, as do Singapore-based church leaders who travel to minister in neighbouring countries. For many churches, these short-term and non-residential approaches form the bulk of their missions strategies.

Such non-residential approaches are probably most appropriate when there is an existing indigenous church that can be engaged in some form of partnership (some church leaders call these "church-to-church partnerships"). In places where there is no such a local church, long-term sending strategies are probably most appropriate because a deeper level of cultural intelligence and local knowledge is required for pioneering work.

Indigenous Partnerships

Creating partnerships with indigenous ministries in different nations can be a highly effective missions strategy, and many churches are involved in such partnerships. Church leaders note that if it is a well-balanced and well-managed partnership, the indigenous partner can guide the work with cultural understanding and the Singapore church can be a tremendous source of resources and training. Part of the appeal of the indigenous partnerships approach is that there is a relatively quick start-up for missions involvement (when compared to raising long-term missionaries). A partner can be found and adopted relatively quickly and on a relatively small budget.

Like any strategy, this approach needs to be infused with appropriate contextualisation; otherwise, ethnocentric mistakes will be made. Sustainability, patronage and dependency issues also need to be well thought through. This approach cannot be used where there exists neither a national church nor a strong group of believers to partner with, and it is thus less likely to be used with unreached people groups. According to the Joshua Project, 40% of the people groups in the world do not yet have an indigenous community of believing Christians with adequate numbers and resources to evangelise this people (what we consider "unreached").[2]

THREE TRENDS IN SINGAPORE MISSIONS

While the ensuing list is by no means exhaustive, the following trends are shaping the strategic choices of local churches.

Trend 1: *Reduction in Long-Term Sending*

Many leaders in the missions community are concerned that long-term sending is on the decline in Singapore. Hearing from leaders represented in my study, including those from churches and parachurches, the overwhelming feeling is that fewer people are now available for long-term missionary service. It has also become popular for churches to exclusively define their long-term missions programmes in shorter periods of one, two or three years. Some churches have completely eliminated (what was traditionally) the long-term category from their missions programme.

The missionary in such scenarios, therefore, essentially serves for a maximum of a 'single term,' as defined by the traditional long-term, incarnational missionary approach. This observation should not conclude that no place exists for such short-term strategies; however, dialogue is needed to address the cultural intelligence and strategic shortfalls of this approach. Missionaries on such short-term missions are often driven to produce results even before their cultural adjustment and language acquisition have developed sufficiently.

In statistics from the 1990s,[3] Singapore appeared near the top of the list of countries for sending of long-term missionaries. My qualitative study shows wide concern by both agency and church leaders that long-term sending is on the decline in the nation. This is supported by recent quantitative data from the Singapore Centre of Global Missions.[4]

One comment that has been repeated numerous times in various ways was, "I find that fewer and fewer people are going out long-term nowadays. I used to regularly hear people say they were going for missions work, but for the last ten or twenty years, it has been less. It's not a good sign, especially if we are to be the Antioch of Asia. We still need long-term workers." The majority of church and missions leaders I interviewed have pointed to this trend. While there exist patches of interest and activity in long-term missions, these are not in great numbers.

Some church and agency leaders spoke of periods when they perceived that Singapore was doing better, with the implication that we have "lost something" in missions. As one missions pastor said, "In the late 1990s and early 2000s, it was very powerful. I think it shaped many people. Those from that era still talk about the 'good old days'." Another leader echoed these sentiments, "I think that we were more forward [looking] in the 1990s, but now 15 years later, we are somehow not moving forward, but sliding back a little bit." Some missions pastors spoke of this period as being "distracted" and others spoke of a "generation we have lost" to missions. There is a need for a fresh clarion call to long-term missions and missions among the unreached.

Trend 2: The Appeal of "Missions in our Backyard"

A corollary to the first trend is the increased focus on cross-cultural missions in our own backyard. The appeal of this may be because it is a strategy that can still be used with the declining long-term workforce.

Surprisingly, however, in some quarters, there is a belief that there is no longer a necessity for long-term sending. Some imply it is because we now have the 'nations in our backyard.' Others say it is because we have local partners in other nations to collaborate with. One comment in an online conversation among lay believers reflected this school of thought: "There are thousands of foreign workers in Singapore. With this [opportunity] to share the gospel, there is less of a need to send missionaries abroad."

Many others disagree with this conclusion. One church leader criticised the tendency of some churches to focus solely on local missions, "It is very simple: Singapore has five million people. Out of this, how many are Christians? And out of the five million, how many parish churches and Christian organisations are there? So to me, Singapore is not the priority... In neighbouring countries, there are hundreds of millions—over two billion across Asia—who have not heard the gospel. I am looking at those areas." It may not be a situation of local missions or overseas missions, but rather, both are needed.

Trend 3: *Primarily Asia focus*

From my interviews, I found that Singaporean churches are focusing the majority of their missions work in Asia. Many churches have written this scope into their policies, and some have even defined their field of ministry as "anywhere within seven hours' flight of Singapore".[5] There are exceptions to this exclusively Asia focus, but these are few and far between.

The reasons given for this are fairly consistent. One is that church leaders felt there is a natural geographical and cultural proximity, which "makes sense" and enables ready access and efficiency in the process. They even felt there is some intuition that exists when they work in Asia, which may not be present in other cultures. Some feel that they are just not well equipped or resourced enough to go beyond Asia. Others gave more parochial reasons, such as their leadership and congregations will "buy into" the Asian vision more readily.

Interestingly, one of the reasons given by church leaders for this exclusive focus on Asia is that they cannot afford to go beyond Asia. This pragmatic approach is surprising considering the wealth of the nation. While many people complain that the rising cost of living in Singapore is burdensome, the nation has missions resources that stand out in the global landscape. In one network discussion, a church leader challenged this perspective, questioning whether missions should be driven by "economics and from our excess" or from obedience and sacrificial service.

A small number of missions leaders and church pastors felt that it is time to look beyond Asia. As one pastor pointed out, the "Antioch of Asia" title was not meant to restrict us to Asia, but to see workers sent from Asia to all parts of the global harvest. Others also pointed out that Singapore itself would never have been evangelised if European and British missionaries had such restrictions on their vision.

THREE AREAS FOR GROWTH IN SINGAPORE MISSIONS

Along with the sense that Singapore is doing many good things in missions, there is an equally large number of church and agency leaders who recognised that there are more opportunities for growth, if we are to truly be the Antioch of Asia. One agency leader said, "I think Singapore has made great leaps in this area. The statement that you made about the Antioch of Asia – part of it may be true, but part of it isn't."

Issue 1: *Need to Grow in our Cultural Intelligence*

If there is a weakness at the top of the list, it will be the need for our movement to grow in cultural intelligence and strategic missiological thinking. These are consistent themes that emerged from the interviews and almost all the stakeholders cited examples to support their comments.

The ability to work effectively in another culture does not come "naturally". On the contrary, what is intuitively correct in our culture may be completely reversed in another culture. Cultural intelligence, also called CQ, is what helps us avoid what earlier missionary movements had been accused of—ethnocentrism, cultural imperialism and paternalistic approaches. As one missionary said, "I think this happens when people come in and they already have an idea of how things work. They don't study the culture or do things that fit into the culture."

Many interviewees recognised that our productivity-driven Singaporean culture can be a weakness in this area. What has made us a global success in many spheres of endeavour can make us susceptible to errors. One missions pastor put it this way, "A strength can also be a weakness. Our organisation and leadership in hierarchal structures can be strengths, but they can also become weaknesses if we go into the different cultures and tell them this is the way you must do missions. There is a tendency for the Singapore church to give orders more than partnering."

Missions pastors, agency leaders and missionaries themselves spoke of having observed churches trying to take a "short runway." This implies haste in the process and expectations of quick results. Others spoke of "taking shortcuts." A senior pastor recounted that he had observed Singapore churches using money in very inappropriate ways, simply because they wanted to see quick results. Another direct-send missions pastor said, "When I go to the mission field, I see my missionary doing it the Singaporean style. I have to deliberately stop him and tell him, "You cannot do it the Singaporean style!" The same direct-send missions pastor spoke of his struggle with how to guide his missionaries when they have problems, as well as his need for help in strategic thinking.

Issue 2: Not Going to the Hard Places

During the interviews, it was evident that the majority of churches, especially direct-send churches, are limiting the difficulty level of the mobilisation projects they take on because they recognise the limits of their local church capacity and experience. One missions leader used the term, "low-hanging fruit", to describe the goals that many churches reach for. Another agency specialist spoke of the tendency for many churches in Singapore to "cherry pick" by going to places that are likely to give quick results.

One church leader pondered, "Maybe in the first 50 years, it was good to go to the easy places. We went to places that we were more familiar with ... but in the coming phase, I would ask, 'What are other more strategic directions we can move into?' I would say it is unreached peoples. That is our main challenge." It may be that our young missions movement needs help to go to the hard places, and that is where partnership in missions must play a greater role.

Issue 3: Need to Learn from the Past

The "whole church taking the gospel to the whole world" nature of global missions, means that integrating the diversity of the global workforce is a priority. Singapore's convenient position between the East and West makes it a good place to wrestle with how to effectively mobilise Asians and integrate with older Western missionary movements. Cultural intelligence is now needed on multicultural teams, training needs must be customised and good cross-cultural communication is required if Asians are going to partner well with the rest of the world. As Fung points out, there is a necessity for both Western agencies to recognise that adjustments are needed to accommodate the Asian missionary force and Asian leaders to "humbly acknowledge with gratitude the contribution of the Western missionaries" (65–76).

One agency board member commented on our need to learn from the past mistakes of other movements, "What I want to see is missionary sending agencies within denominations learning from the lessons of missionaries sent from the West... I think we need to learn from those lessons and not repeat the mistakes." The Singapore movement is still relatively young, so it is important to make sure that local churches and mission agencies are connected to the wider global missions movement. One way to do this is through more effective partnerships.

Caution: Guard Against Ethnocentric Approaches

We urgently need to ensure that Asian missionary movements do not adopt ethnocentric approaches. These are often driven by hasty methods and expectations of quick productivity. The risk of this is heightened by the move toward short-term methods that do not give missionaries sufficient time to grow their cultural intelligence. The lack of partnership with specialists and the assumption that being Asian gives us specific local intelligence can unknowingly leave us at greater risk of exposure to ethnocentric approaches. As one Singaporean missionary said, "Churches in Singapore, perhaps because of their higher cultural and contextual understanding, assume that they have more specific understanding [than they actually do]. They don't have as much contextual understanding and that is when trouble can happen."

Tan writes, there is a "danger of an Asian ethnocentrism, which claims that this is the Asia Pacific Century and that leadership in mission belongs to the Asian church." Rather, he goes on to present a list of challenges facing Asian missions, concluding, "Implicitly, the list sets out the case against newer Asian missions movements which prefer to do mission without partnering with all the sending structures from the West" (54).

THE STATE OF MISSIONS PARTNERSHIP IN SINGAPORE

Church leaders in Singapore are taking full advantage of the opportunities that the enablers in the current environment offer, using a mixture of methods to initiate a broad cross-section of missions projects. It is interesting that many of those same pastors view missions agency partnership as an option, rather than a necessity.

Why Churches Continue to Partner with Missions Agencies

A significant number of churches are moving to a direct-send approach in missions mobilisation, but a good proportion still see value in partnering with agencies. They recognise that the local church is a generalist by nature and necessity, and that missions agencies can provide the specialist help required for the complex nature of cross-cultural missions.

One of the most common reasons local church leaders felt that it was important to partner with missions agencies is the expertise and experience they provide. They felt that, in general, the local church is unable to properly handle the work of missions by itself, particularly in the area of sending long-term missionaries, and especially to hard places. Pastors from churches with decades of missions experience spoke of unexpected difficulties in their past attempts to do missions without agency help. They expressed reluctance to try again given a choice. Agencies help to fill the gaps, guide the process, share the load and equip the people.

Even pastors who are strongly in favour of the direct-send model acknowledged that caring for a missionary in the field is difficult and that the field structure which missions agencies provide is one of their great advantages. As one direct-sending missions pastor said, "I think [our church] handles member care quite well, but we may not be able to handle the destination well... This is where the field of knowledge is beyond our church." Even pastors who prefer the direct-send method acknowledged that the model is not as appropriate for the hard places.

Church leaders recognise that mission agencies have "tried and tested models." One missions chairman said, "Agencies are not new; they have been around for a long time and have built upon their failures. Agencies are populated by people who have often been in the field themselves at some point."

Why Churches Move Away from Agency Sending

In a sense, when a church chooses to direct-send, it is choosing to create its own missions agency within the structure of the local church. Some churches come to the same point where they feel that they are large enough and rich enough to direct-send their own missionaries.

One of the main reasons given by many churches for their direct-send strategy (and often the first one cited) is the sense of engagement, ownership and excitement the church feels, when compared to sending though an agency partnership. Being in the mobilisation "driver's seat" gives the church a sense that "we are doing it." They feel that it gives them a stronger ability to generate interest and commitment from their congregation. As one missions pastor said, "I think if we can give that sense of ownership, it may just be able to drive people's interest. So if we can say that this is our missionary and we have a vision to do it on the field, I think we can mobilise people and resources."

Another reason church leaders give for wanting to drive their own missions programmes is disappointment with past attempts to engage with agencies. They spoke of a lack of good fit and flexibility in the organisations they tried to work with. It was difficult to find a common ground. One missions pastor said, "It is not that we don't want to be in partnership, but the agendas are very different, so it is very difficult to come to an agreement without compromising what we wanted to do."

Words such as "red tape" were also used by church leaders to describe some agencies. They did, however, acknowledge that this varied from agency to agency and person to person, even within the partnering agency. One former missionary who now serves as a church staff spoke of the "take it all or nothing" approach of some agencies, which can seem inflexible. He said, "Direct-send churches can go where they want and they can do what they want, with more flexibility than missions agency programmes."

The Need to Redefine Partnership in Missions

There is a need to renegotiate what partnership in missions looks like. We need to find common ground. It has been pointed out that the primary reason for meeting, relationship and collaboration between local churches and mission agencies has traditionally been the long-term sending of missionaries. Hence, as one pastor put it, with the reduction of long-term sending and the move toward direct-sending, the "glue" between churches and agencies is reducing.

At the same time, other churches are asking for help and recognising that agencies have competencies and processes that they could tap into. Pastors are looking for "consultants" to assist them in their missions programmes. There was an assertion by a missions pastor that having *the desire* to do missions is different from knowing how to *go about it*. He felt that many churches have a strong desire to be involved in missions, but they "have no clue" how to implement their vision. Even strong churches can benefit from receiving help from consultants who would guide with their experience and know-how.

CONCLUSION

Like tension in a marriage, there exists confusion in the relationship between churches and agencies regarding how they can move forward in a mutually respectful and satisfying relationship. The time is right for an appropriate dialogue about the shape of missions partnership in Singapore.

The reality is that the world is changing, and both agencies and churches need to adjust their approaches. The trends and challenges identified in the Singaporean missions movement are by no means unique in the global landscape. However, the intensity in which they are being expressed in this small nation may well be a unique opportunity for experimentation and innovation in partnership, and we may eventually find emerging models that can serve the wider global missions movement. I am praying for more intentional strategic dialogue about missions partnership. The end result will hopefully be a more robust missions movement with excellent missions collaboration and efforts, which will have a greater impact around the world.

"Now what?" we may ask. The next chapters of this book continue with the principles of partnership, research findings, and a model for more effective church-agency relationships. While these are necessary foundations, the reality is that partnership is born in relationship and dialogue. Part 2 of this book is the fruit of many such hours of dialogue among a group of church and missions agency leaders who applied, validated and strengthened the research findings and model that you are about to learn. The process has built a robust foundation that we hope will support a move toward greater interdependency between mission agencies and local churches.

chapter 2

BIBLICAL, THEOLOGICAL & HISTORICAL FOUNDATIONS

Ivan Liew

After taking stock of the state of missions partnerships between churches and agencies in our context, we are ready to continue our thinking on biblical, theological and historical foundations. If you wish to skip this chapter, know that later parts of the book will refer back to concepts explained here. You can come back at a later time, but before proceeding to chapter 3, read the concluding section in this chapter, "Summary of Partnership Values", which contains the four partnership values derived from this chapter.

The resurgence of interest in the Trinity is now finding its way past academic and theological discussions to the practice of ministry. The Trinitarian relationship is also relevant to the topic of church-agency relationships and so this chapter will deal with the theological basis of partnerships that is grounded in the Trinity. Many people intuitively know that relationships are critical in an organisational partnership, but a Trinitarian grounding will explain why this is so and expand upon the nature of these relationships in ways that will guide us to form stronger partnerships.

We will also discuss the biblical and historical foundations of churches and missions agencies. This background will later be useful to understand why and how we can value one another and more effectively conduct our partnerships today.

THE TRINITARIAN BASIS FOR PARTNERSHIP

God is inherently relational within his triune being, and since he created mankind in his own image, Trinitarian theology speaks directly to his design concerning how we are to conduct ourselves in relationships and partnerships.

Relationships between Christians within a church are often used as a measure of unity and spiritual health within the local body. Similarly, this barometer applies to partnership relationships between Christian organisations as a measure of the spiritual unity with the larger Church. Though an organisation may demonstrate relationship and diversity within itself, practising Trinitarian relationships at the inter-organisational level through missional partnerships further demonstrates God's character.

Partnership is a concept integral to the very Trinitarian nature of God, for there is partnership within the Godhead. When we address God, we speak to a relational community of three divine persons (Ross 146). In this manner, understanding the Trinitarian relationship within the Godhead will help us to understand God's design for our own inter-organisational partnerships.

The Trinity and Partnership Relationships

The very fabric and nature of a Christian partnership must be different from that of the non-Christian world. To say that our partnership is Trinitarian would be to say that our Christian partnership displays God's character in its relational practice.

Churches and missions agencies are also *one* and *different* at the same time, similar to the Trinity. Our organisations are one in Christ and one in his body, yet we are clearly different in our purposes and structures. Being *one* and *different* is not mutually exclusive, for our differences can make our unity all the more beautiful. The Father, Son and Holy Spirit demonstrate this simultaneous oneness and difference in their coexistence, thus providing this perfect example of how people and organisations in the global Church can be one and different at the same time.

David Cunningham describes this oneness and difference as "simultaneous multiplicity", which he likens to music where different harmonious notes are played together to form music. Extending this analogy further, in musical polyphony, two or more independent melodies can be played simultaneously, creating different sequences that overlap, yet are still enacted as a single musical piece. Beautiful choral pieces and instrumental ensembles result from independent melodies that are beautifully woven together (126–28).

This analogy illustrates the oneness and difference that can be evident in church-agency partnerships. A local church and missions agency each have their own vision, yet they minister together as the body of Christ for the one mission of God. In the same way that a single musical piece brings forth joy to the listener, so inter-organisational partnership glorifies God and brings forth joy when the Church lives and ministers in harmony. This kind of Trinitarian unity leaves room for being different in structure, yet affirms being bound in a relationship of love, sharing mission and vision.

Trinitarian Values that Guide Partnerships

The gospel of John is sometimes referred to as the gospel of love because of its focus on this theme. One of the aspects of love that Mark Shaw discerns in John's gospel is how it describes the love relationship between the Father, Son and Holy Spirit—all three members of the Trinity. He describes four ways that the persons in the Godhead treat one another. These four aspects of the Trinitarian relationship can be values that guide us in our partnerships:

1. Full equality with one another

2. Glad submission to one another

3. Enjoyment of intimacy with one another

4. Mutual deference to one another (62–64).

These characteristics of relationship provide invaluable guidance on how local churches and missions agencies should conduct themselves in partnerships. Consider how these values are demonstrated in John's gospel.

Unprecedented in his time, Jesus called God his own Father, making himself equal to God (John 5:18). He affirmed this equality when he said, "If you knew me, you would know my Father also" (John 8:19). Full equality within the Godhead did not preclude mutual deference and submission among members of the Trinity. Relationships within the Godhead do not evidence attempts to balance the roles, but display a perfect coexistence of the different roles, demonstrating the perfect divine family relationship. Local churches and missions organisations should view each other as equal in value with regard to the missions task, honouring and respecting each other as needed members within the global church labouring in God's kingdom. Full equality does not mean the same roles, for just as the Father, Son and Holy Spirit exercise different functions, so do the local churches and missions agencies.

Mutual deference and glad submission are revealed in the Godhead as perfectly coexisting with this equality. Jesus demonstrates this when he contemplates his own mission and death. "For this reason the Father loves me, because I lay down my life that I may take it up again. No one takes it from me, but I lay it down of my own accord. I have authority to lay it down, and I have authority to take it up again. This charge I have received from my Father" (John 10:17-18).

While the Son acts under the Father's will, he does so with autonomy and of his own accord because the Father has deferred power to the Son. The Son exercises his mission under the loving overview of the Father. In the same vein, Timothy Tennent writes that "the Father imparts all authority to Jesus" (see Matt. 28:18), signifying that the deference of power and giving of authority are foundational for the church's Trinitarian missiology (157).

This divine interaction of mutual deference and glad submission especially informs relationships where one party has oversight of another and grants this other party autonomy and trust to accomplish the mission. The church is called to join God's mission; thus, the church has theological primacy in missions but defers its human and financial resources to the missions agency, in order that the agency may take action and better accomplish the cross-cultural aspect of mission. The missions agency has authority and autonomy, which are gladly given by the church. Such an arrangement is only possible with trust and understanding, and is best accomplished through a relationship of love, rather than one of legal documents and contracts.

This relationship is made possible by enjoyment of intimacy with one another, one of the four characteristics of the Trinitarian relationship. Trinitarian theology points toward this characteristic simultaneously, being both a necessary prerequisite and a fruit of commitment to modelling partnerships on the Godhead.

On a personal level, this understanding translates to joyful fellowship among leaders of like-minded organisations as being both a preface and an outflow of missions partnerships. On the organisational level, both churches and agencies enjoy the intimacy of fellowship as they grow together, see fruit in ministry and observe their resources effectively employed for God's kingdom. Christian partnerships are not merely contractual obligations but intimate connections within the body of Christ. As in an organic body, connections between members of Christ's body are marked by interconnectedness and interdependence (Bonk 130).

Thus far, we have seen how the divine relationship within the Godhead exhibits all four characteristics of full equality, mutual deference, enjoyment of intimacy and glad submission, providing a guiding basis for partnership relationships.

Trinitarian Values for Missions

Jesus prays to the Father for the comprehensive inclusion of all Christians into this relationship through the Spirit abiding in the Church. "I do not ask for these only, but also for those who will believe in me through their word, that they may all be one, just as you, Father, are in me, and I in you, that they also may be in us, *so that the world may believe that you have sent me.* The glory that you have given me I have given to them, that they may be one even as we are one, I in them and you in me, that they may become perfectly one, *so that the world may know that you sent me and loved them even as you loved me*" (John 17:20-23, *emphasis mine*).

Therefore, a key result of all Christians' inclusion in the Trinitarian relationship is the proclamation of Christ's mission. This fact further drives home the relevance of the Trinity to partnerships between churches and missions agencies. We will now continue by turning our attention to biblical and historical perspectives, which will eventually be blended together to form the *Relational Model of Church-Agency Partnerships* that integrates these values and principles.

HISTORICAL REVIEW OF MISSIONS PARTNERSHIPS

The purpose of a brief historical review of missions is to understand the crucial role that specialist organisations such as missions agencies have played in the expansion of the Church. With very few exceptions, the phenomenon of local churches involving themselves successfully in direct-sending cross-cultural missions is a very recent phenomenon. In contrast, the partnership between churches and specialist missions organisations have been the historical norm. While church-agency partnerships have frequently been fraught with tension and suboptimal practices, history has shown them to be the recipients of God's blessing of fruitfulness.

Missionary Bands in the First Century

The New Testament records that the Holy Spirit directed the church to form missionary bands in order to conduct missionary endeavours. Acts 13:1-3 records how the Holy Spirit directed the church in Antioch to set apart Paul and Barnabas for missionary work. From this text, we see God calling missionaries into ministry and a community of believers affirming their call and sending them off. The resulting missionary bands of the New Testament were thus formed outside of local church structures, but Paul never saw himself as being totally separate from the local church.

In Acts 14:27-28, Paul returns to Antioch and "declared all that God had done for them, and how he had opened a door of faith to the Gentiles. And they remained no little time with the disciples". The biblical record gives the sense of sharing important information and extended fellowship, as opposed to a relationship where church leaders in Antioch directed the ministry of the apostolic band. Even in Acts 15, when issues surrounding Gentile conversions were raised to the Jerusalem Council, Paul and Barnabas related "signs and wonders that God had done through them" (Acts 15:12), joining in the robust debate around the issue of whether Gentiles believers should be circumcised.

These instances demonstrate an autonomous and interdependent relationship between missionary bands and the local church, a relationship that extended into the epistles where Paul connected back to churches he had planted, such as the groups of believers in Philippi. Thus, the missionary bands were autonomous in that they made most of their own strategic and daily decisions, but acted in conjunction with the local church, reporting back to it when appropriate, and exchanging pastoral care and mutual encouragement.

Missionary bands were functional precursors to non-ecclesiastical organisations involved in missionary work, such as the monastic movement in medieval times and missions societies in modern times. However, these three structures are not historically connected even though they were functionally similar. In other words, monasticism did not historically derive from missionary bands, and missions societies cannot trace their historical roots to either the monastic movement or missionary bands, though they were functionally connected. All of these groups worked alongside the local church for the missionary expansion of the body of Christ.

The Monastic Movement

By the fifth century, the monastic movement was well underway, though it was sometimes viewed suspiciously by the diocesan structure of Rome. The rapid growth and widespread adoption of the Rule of Saint Benedict remarkably integrated missionary concerns into monasticism, which was strongly ascetic up to that time.

Benedictine monasteries would have seemed, to modern observers, more like a community of monastic missionaries than the stereotypical reclusive monks. The monastery cultivated soil, fed the poor, healed the sick, preached the gospel and gave spiritual direction to the young monks who increasingly flocked to Benedict (Schaff 216–20). The Benedictine monks chose relationships in community over a life of solitude in order to deepen their spiritual walk. Holistic missions to the surrounding community overflowed from discipleship in their own community. Benedictine monastic orders sent forth large numbers of missionaries who were prepared for hardship, trained to minister to people, equipped to convert communities to Christ, and passionate to disciple communities guided by the Benedictine rule.

In centuries to come, monastic orders again produced the most number of centres of learning, bishops and missionaries, to guide and grow the Church in the West and in their expansion efforts to Asia and South America (Schaff 224–26). The Benedictines, the Cluny reform, the Cistercians, the Friars and the Jesuits were all part of this monastic movement that made immense contributions to the building of the Roman Catholic Church.

Originally birthed out of an ascetic desire for deeper personal spirituality, the monastic movement became the strongest missionary force of the Church throughout the middle ages and remains so for the Roman Catholic Church today. Monasteries, with their specialist nature and structural separation from the diocesan church, were able to develop people with the missionary zeal and spiritual fervour necessary for participation in the expansion of God's kingdom. Though Rome had managed to synthesise the diocesan structure and monastic structure into a fruitful partnership, the relationship was not without tension and rivalry.

Protestant Reformation and the Lack of Missions

By the sixteenth century, the Reformation was underway. The Protestant focus was on the renewal of the Church, and energies were expended looking inward, debating right theology, building ecclesiastical structures and warding off opponents. None of the resulting Protestant movements considered foreign missionary advancement to unreached peoples for hundreds of years.

Winter notes that while the various Protestant movements formed congregational church structures to replace the Roman Catholic diocesan structure, none formed any renewing structures apart from the congregation that mirrored the Catholic monastic orders. He argues that neglecting to build structures to serve the missionary function of the monastic orders resulted in the Protestants having no mechanism for missions for three hundred years (99). During these three centuries, the early Reformation movement focused on congregational life and did not consider foreign missions a necessary part of the new church.

Analogous to how asceticism birthed missionary monasticism in the fifth century, pietism gave rise to Protestant missions. In the seventeenth century, Philipp Spener began seeking deeper spirituality and renewal within the Lutheran church by forming groups within churches that would be committed to learn more of Scriptures (Walker

587). These pietistic revivals grew and became convinced of God's call to the lost, giving rise to the earliest Protestant missionary societies, including the Moravian Missions in 1732, which emanated from the Moravian Brethren (Eckman 68–70).

Moravians and the Modern Missions Movement

As the Moravians gained missionary sending experience, they developed detailed instructions for their missionaries and trained them for their work. This extraordinary integration of specialist missions function and the general life of the church was a new phenomenon. Entire communities and families, not just a few pious individuals, were devoted to the missionary expansion of the faith. Its purposefulness of focus resembled that of some of the monastic orders, but this time with an entire church community, including laity and clergy, involved in the task. While the Moravians were not the first Protestant missionary society, they can be said to be the first Protestant missionary church (Hutton 226).

Fifty years later, William Carey helped to spark the English Evangelical Revival when he published *An Enquiry* in 1792. The book reviewed what the Catholic monastic orders did in the past and what Protestants had accomplished up to that time. He wrote, "None of the moderns have equalled the Moravian Brethren in this good work" (16). Soon after, the *Particular Baptist Society for Propagating the Gospel among the Heathen* was formed.

This missionary society first sent Carey to India in 1800, where he established himself with five other families, organising themselves in an intentional community with strategies that Carey acknowledged he learned from previous successful Moravian examples (Schattschneider 9–11). Carey's life example and teachings sparked a missionary awakening. Fed by numerous revivals, the number of missions societies grew rapidly.

Kenneth Scott Latourette describes the Christianity of this period as strongly missionary, with people in nation after nation where the gospel was being preached not only becoming adherents, but forming their own missions societies and becoming missionary sending forces themselves (94). Missions organisations fulfilled critical needs, such as providing legitimacy to a missionary, missions awareness to churches, wider publicity and fundraising that was necessary for the success of missions (Wuthnow 99–103). This model of cross-cultural missions remained the widespread norm until the twentieth century, when other methods of missionary sending began to appear.

CHURCHES IN MISSIONS TODAY

Much of the missionary effort in the modern missions movement has been conducted by missions societies or agencies. Denominations and local churches have been slower to respond to the call to bring the gospel to other nations, focusing efforts instead on ministering to their members and those in their immediate vicinity. The situation is changing, however, with increasing numbers of churches becoming convinced that they must be directly involved in world evangelisation and desiring more direct involvement in the mission field (Pierson 149–50).

Robert Wuthnow reports that 84% of US evangelical church members say that their congregation supports missionaries abroad. Corresponding figures for mainline Protestants and Catholics are also high at 73% and 69%, respectively (149).

American Megachurches in Missions

Robert J. Priest, Douglas Wilson and Adelle Johnson conducted research specifically focused on North American megachurches' involvement in missions. The reason for this focus was that, though Christianity is shifting to the global south, much of the structure and resources remain in the global north. Further, megachurches have great influence on missions patterns, sometimes even more than denominational leaders or missions executives and missiologists (97–102).

While American megachurches continue to send large numbers of career missionaries, support for them is decreasing when compared to total expenditure and newer missions priorities, such as short-term missions, poverty relief and partnerships with churches in the developing world. Approximately 40% of megachurches either were neutral or disagreed with the statement that career missionaries are strategically important and should be generously supported.

While megachurches reported strong increases in average attendance, total church income and participation in short-term missions over the previous five years, the number of supported career missionaries only barely increased. In fact, supported career missionaries experienced a relative decrease in proportion to total ministry and resources (Priest, Wilson, and Johnson 97–98). While the authors did not report on what proportion of missionaries were sent through agencies, this congregational softening of support for long-term missions is certainly a factor in the changing landscape of partnerships between megachurches and missions agencies.

Philip Jenkins has described how Christianity is shifting to the global south toward new centres of Christianity in Latin America, Africa and Asia (8–10). Complementing this observation, Priest's

US megachurch research reveals that megachurches are primarily engaging in short-term missions in precisely these most Christian countries. For example, North American short-term missions are often conducted in Guatemala, Uganda and Kenya—countries with high percentages of Christians.

When Priest, Wilson and Johnson compared these findings with David B. Barrett's typology that distinguishes between the most and least evangelised countries (Barrett et al. 23–25), they discovered that 82% of megachurches focus on countries that are the most Christian, and only 6% focus on countries that are the least Christian. This leads to the conclusion that megachurch short-term missions "is largely a paradigm of partnership, connecting Christians in resource-rich regions of the world with Christians in regions of poverty in joint projects of witness and service" (Priest, Wilson, and Johnson 99). This significant trend of global missions is moving on a different track from traditional missions agencies, which are focused on reaching the unreached and mobilising more long-term missionaries to be sent to these people groups.

The Direction of Missions Partnerships

Recent missions history reveals that local churches are taking up the responsibility for cross-cultural missions with vigour and a commendable sense of ownership. While some churches eschew traditional missions and partnerships with agencies, opting instead for direct-sending, these churches are not rejecting partnership altogether. Instead, they are partnering with national churches and organisations. The tendency is for these cross-cultural activities to be from resource-rich countries to resource-poor nations where there is already a Christian presence.

In contrast, a second group of churches continues to send missionaries through missions agencies. They value long-term missionaries and missions to unreached and least-reached peoples. While this book is clearly written for this second group, the challenge remains for missions agencies to consider how they can be relevant to churches in the first group. These leaders may not desire a traditional sending model, but they not infrequently request consultation or assistance in member care or crisis management.

Past arguments about the validity of parachurch organisations and their role in relation to the local church have given way to widespread agreement that both churches and missions agencies are valuable and needed in the global missions endeavour. Even churches whose missions policy does not include missions agencies generally acknowledge their contribution and sometimes even ask for their assistance.

BIBLICAL CENTRALITY OF THE CHURCH & LEGITIMACY OF THE MISSIONS AGENCY

The previous sections in this chapter have dealt with why missions partnerships are so important and the manner in which we are to conduct them, from both biblical and theological perspectives. As we apply these to partnerships between churches and missions agencies, the thorny questions of "Who is in charge?" and "Who does missions belong to?" are raised.

While later chapters in Part 2 of this book will present a nuanced answer to these questions according to different areas of missions partnerships, we first need to define the more primary aspects of legitimacy and role of the missions agency and the local church.

Dual Legitimacy of Church and Agency

Ralph Winter first coined the terms, "modality" and "sodality", to describe the separate structures of the church and parachurch organisations, including missions agencies. Winter argues that both structures are legitimate and needed for world evangelisation (121). Regarding the relationship and legitimacy of churches and parachurch organisations, a wide variety of views exist, ranging from the illegitimacy of parachurch groups to temporary legitimacy for such groups and dual legitimacy for both structures (White 65–66).

Missions organisations are a subset of these parachurch groups, and the majority view has gravitated toward a dual legitimacy for missions agencies and local churches as essential parts of the body of Christ working together in global missions. Most would recognise specialist, non-congregational Christian ministries to be essential in the expansion of the kingdom of God, with the ecclesiological differentiation of them not being a church in the sense that they are not a local congregation of believers (Lausanne Committee 11). This understanding differentiates, but does not undermine, a missions organisation's status, for one cannot refute the historical effectiveness of missions organisations, whether in the monastic movement or the Protestant modern missions movement.

Church and Agency in Tension

While dual legitimacy of church and parachurch organisations is generally agreed upon, more recent discussions have dealt with the contentious issue of the status of the church as compared to the parachurch. In the Lausanne Consultation's handbook "Cooperating in World Evangelization", John Stott suggests that the church/parachurch friction reflects the "age-old tension between authority and freedom." Stott and the committee suggests that, for specialist organisations, "independence of the church is bad, co-operation with the church is better, service as an arm of the church is best."

Serving the church is not the specific issue that causes tension, but Stott correctly points out the root issues as that of authority and freedom. Many leaders of missions organisations would agree that their desire is to serve the local church while simultaneously hoping that sufficient autonomy is built into the partnership. They believe that serving the church does not relegate the missions agency to a subordinate role that is less valued as compared to the church.

Larry Sharp, a missionary and the director of a missions organisation, writes that he is "committed to the local church and its primary role in world missions" (78–79). Steve Beirn, a missions pastor of a large church, argues that the New Testament, and in particular Acts 13, depicts the "priority and authority of the local church as the mediating sending agent under the headship of Christ" (109-11).

Whether made by an agency director or a missions pastor, statements with reference to the primary role, priority or authority of the church can cause unease when missions organisations feel that churches may use it in an inappropriate manner to exercise undue authority over them.

In another example, John Hammett, a professor of systematic theology, argues that parachurch organisations are "legitimate and valuable partners with churches in ministry; but possess a status subordinate to that of churches." He bases this on a claim of "theological priority for the church" (203–5). Once again, though missions organisations may be thankful that their value is recognised and while their leaders agree that they should serve the church, it is understandable that having a subordinate status to a local church that claims theological priority may not sit well with them.

Agency leaders desire that their organisations are not only valued, but equally valued in their missions contribution. In expressing this desire, they have sometimes argued that the missions organisation is as equally "church" as the local church. Metcalf and Hirsch write, "The church in its apostolic, missionary form is just as equally 'church' as the church in its local parish form" (28). Such views, in turn, cause church leaders unease for many of them see the local church as having a status that is biblically and theologically unique from the missions organisations. How can church and agency leaders reconcile their views?

While church and agency leaders may express certain theological nuances differently, it is critical to note that the desired endpoint is often remarkably the same. For example, in the sentences immediately following his potentially contentious statement that missions organisations are "as equally 'church' as the church in its local parish form," Metcalf and Hirsch say, "God never designed or intended either to do the work of the other. The evidence from history is abundant that whenever these two structures work cooperatively and interdependently, the Christian movement thrives and moves forward" (28). Speaking from the context of the United Kingdom, Bryan Knell similarly states that churches need the experience and expertise of agencies, and that agencies should encourage churches to be "at the heart or at the centre" of missions (53–60). This cooperative interdependence is the same endpoint that church leaders desire for healthy church-agency partnerships.

Biblical Centrality and Equal Value

We in Churches and Missions Agencies Together (CMAT) have sufficiently resolved these tensions among ourselves by adopting the view of legitimacy of the missions agency as an equal and a valued partner in missions work with the local church, and the local church as having biblical centrality in world evangelisation. Biblical centrality of the church does not mean that the missions agency is subject to the local church for governing decisions, but rather that the local church must play a central role when sending missionaries through missions agency.

Having a central role means that a local church cannot abdicate its responsibilities in world evangelisation, and neither can a missions agency operate independently from the local church. We have found that this language guides and strengthens our partnership relationship. We have therefore moved away from phrases such as "primacy or priority of the local church", Hammett's description of agencies as having "subordinate status", and Metcalf's statement of organisations as being as equally church as local churches. We note that these authors, and most writing on church-agency partnerships, arise from a North-American context. Among the CMAT working group in Singapore, churches do not feel that we need to stress on the primacy of the church and agencies do not need to be seen as equally church in order to be equally valued in missions partnership.

Taken together, dual legitimacy and biblical centrality means that the church and missions agency equally value each other in their missions partnership, and that the missions agency seeks to serve the church with neither organisation as a secondary or subordinate partner. Though the church is biblically central in missions, it defers to the missions agency in certain matters just as the Father, who is the head, defers authority to the Son (John 10:17-18).

SUMMARY OF PARTNERSHIP VALUES

The growing awareness and recognition of the importance of partnerships indicates that it is timely to develop a model of church-agency partnerships that can guide good practices in this murky arena. The next chapter, which focuses on a research study on such partnerships, will explain how such a model was developed and put into practice.

For now, we remind ourselves that the biblical, theological and historical review covered in this chapter provides us with the underlying theology of relationship between the local church and missions agency. This theology draws not only extensively from the Trinitarian relationship, but also the biblical role of the church and the historical efficacy of the agency in missions. We can distil the principles into the following four partnership values, which will be further built upon in Chapters 4 and 5.

1.   Biblical centrality of the church

2.   Equal value of church and agency in missions

3.   Glad submission and mutual deference

4.   Joyful fellowship and encouragement

These four values will undergird the *Relational Model of Church-Agency Partnerships* that was developed through a research study conducted in Woodlands Evangelical Free Church, Singapore. In the next chapter, we will turn our attention to how this research was conducted and the findings that arose.

chapter 3

A RESEARCH STUDY ON CHURCH-AGENCY PARTNERSHIPS

Ivan Liew

When I first took up the role as missions pastor in Woodlands Evangelical Free Church (Woodlands EFC)[6], Singapore, I stepped into a ministry that had already built a strong positive culture of partnerships with missions agencies. Both lay and full-time ministry leaders before me had built this over many years, and I set about trying to build upon the good foundations that had been laid while ascending the steep learning curve of what it meant to be a missions pastor.

We were sending a number of our members as missionaries through several agencies, and whenever I spoke to their national directors, they would thank me for my church being a good partner. I would smile, nod and listen intently as I tried to gather information on what good missions partnership meant. As time passed, I observed that good partnerships were vital yet uncommon occurrences in missions circles.

When I tried to learn more about what definitively made for good partnerships between churches and missions agencies, I found a general agreement that partnerships for world evangelisation were urgently needed. However, the amount of writing on the topic was relatively small, with shorter articles rather than books that dealt thoroughly with what church-agency partnerships entail. Theological articles on the broader church and parachurch relationship existed, while specific writing on the church and missions agency in a sending partnership was scarce. Shorter articles presented various opinions based on experiences, more often from the missions agency side of the relationship.

None of the writing that was specific to managing the church-agency partnership was based on research data gathered in a structured process, nor were they published in peer-reviewed journals. The variety of opinions had not yet coalesced into a unified body of knowledge that practitioners widely agree upon.

A RESEARCH OPPORTUNITY

Therefore, when I had the opportunity to conduct a research study as part of my doctorate of ministry at Asbury Theological Seminary, I decided on the topic of church-agency partnerships. I chose this, largely because I wanted to better understand what a good partnership meant and how to conduct such a relationship. To make the research manageable, I focused the scope on optimising missionary care and mobilisation in a sending partnership between the church and missions agency.

Since my ministry was in Singapore and my church had a 20-year history of partnerships with missions agencies, the research took the form of a case study of my own church's partnerships with several agencies and the experiences of the missionaries that were currently sent through them. By examining these partnerships, I hoped to determine a set of good practices for church-agency relationships. Ideally, these would be guidelines on what churches and agencies should do for optimal missionary care and mobilisation. These would be agreed upon by both agency leaders and church leaders, and backed by the experience of missionaries. In this manner, research data from a variety of sources would support these good practice guidelines.

RESEARCH METHOD

Woodlands EFC had formed partnerships with three missions organisations in Singapore, through which we had sent two married couples and three singles. First, the research aimed to uncover the current practice of missions partnerships between Woodlands EFC and these missions agencies. We would intentionally pause and reflect on what we had done and have been doing over the past six to 20 years of the organisations' partnership relationship. We would determine both the nature of the partnership relationship and the specifics of current practice. Data were gathered primarily through semi-structured interviews with the national directors of the three missions agencies.

The research would next ascertain how effective these partnership practices have been in mobilising missionaries from Woodlands EFC and in ensuring effective member care of its missionaries. This was achieved by comparing the past and current partnership practices with the personal experiences of our missionaries. Each of the seven missionaries (two couples and three singles) were interviewed for this purpose. Analysing the resulting data allowed me to see how the different practices of the agencies affected our missionaries, and also how the changing practices of our church over time impacted them.

Finally, principles were distilled into a guideline of best practices for partnerships and local churches. Eventually, this took the form of *REMCAP*, the *Relational Model for Church-Agency Partnerships* (see chapter 4). This model was validated with all the missions agency directors in one focus group and all the missionaries in a second focus group. After the research study was completed, the model was shared with a wider group of churches and missions agencies in Singapore, which further validated the work. This pilot working group became Churches and Missions Agencies Together (CMAT) and this book is the result of our collaborative work.

The results of the research study can be summarised into three key findings: (1) what ingredients constitute a church-agency partnership, (2) areas of mobilisation that are lacking in partnership and (3) the respective roles in member care that churches and agencies are most effective in. Finally, the study ties these together in *REMCAP*, which serves to guide churches and agencies in good practice guidelines.

FIVE INGREDIENTS OF CHURCH-AGENCY PARTNERSHIP

The missions agencies in this study varied in size, partnership practice, and length and depth of relationship with Woodlands EFC. Despite this variation of partnership relationship, five concepts were common among the responses of all the agency leaders when describing church-agency partnership practice—both with Woodlands EFC and other churches. Like a recipe, these five concepts constitute the key ingredients of a church-agency partnership: people, relationships, vision, ministry philosophy and finances.

People and Relationships

People and relationships were two of the ingredients that appeared in all the agency leaders' responses. People included agency leaders, church leaders and the missionaries themselves. The agency leaders discussed not so much the position itself, but the actions and character of individuals who held positions and the one-on-one relationships forged with them. Specific references to names, and the quality of personal and professional relationships between these people were more relevant than the identification of a position.

Church-agency partnerships suffered either when a manpower shortage resulted in no person holding a needed position, or when one party in the partnership did not make efforts to develop the relationship with the other. In such cases, the partnership continued, but the relationship was weak. In other instances, a commitment to working together resulted in a deepening of personal relationship between church and agency leaders, and a strengthening of organisational partnership.

Vision and Ministry Philosophy

Vision and ministry philosophy were the next ingredients that emerged in the responses of all three agency leaders. *Vision* can be said to be what the church and agency wishes to achieve through the sending partnership. *Ministry philosophy* is why each organisation does things the way it does, and is thus more fundamental than strategy or the plans made for how goals are accomplished. A church and missions agency need to have their *vision* and *ministry philosophy* aligned in the area of their partnership.

A church and missions agency can still have a successful partnership when inevitable differences arise on how things are to be done. Glad submission and mutual deference are possible in strategy decision when there is agreement on the underlying issue of what is to be achieved (vision), and why our choices and actions are important (ministry philosophy).

For all directors, the key means by which vision and ministry philosophy were shared and built was through personal relationships. However, good relationships in themselves did not guarantee good missions partnerships. As one agency director suggested, more fundamental than relationships is "the like-mindedness of ministry philosophy and the vision of missions, followed by relationship and understanding, which build trust between the church and the agency." Another director emphasised "sharing the vision" and mutual understanding with partner churches.

Finances

Finances was the fifth ingredient for partnerships, as financial and human resources were key assets exchanged between the church and agency in these partnerships. Typically, both the missions agency and the missionary sent through the agency require funds from the church in the partnership. One agency director said that without a pre-existing relationship of trust, church leaders tend to think that the agencies want their money and their people whenever a meeting is requested. Some agencies have a policy of not soliciting money from churches, while another agency leader recognised that *finances* was a difficult area of relationship with churches that needed more of his attention. The sentiments regarding finances expressed by each director were key indicators of the health of a particular partnership they had with a church, whether that was Woodlands EFC or another church being discussed.[7]

Connecting the Ingredients

When discussing these five ingredients, certain connections between these issues became evident. Agency leaders tended to assess the quality and health of the partnership in terms of four ingredients: *relationships, vision, ministry philosophy* and *finances*. Therefore, these four concepts were not only practices, but also means of evaluating whether the partnership was progressing well. The *relationships* ingredient was particularly important, as agency leaders repeatedly referred to the church's relational commitment to the missionary and their relationship with the church, especially the personal interaction with the church's missions leaders. Further, the *relationships* ingredient was used not only to assess the partnership, but also to strengthen other practices. When relationships were positive, the other ingredients of *vision, ministry philosophy* and *finances* could be strengthened through this rapport.

Another connection between the ingredients is how *relationships, vision, ministry philosophy* and *finances* either affect or are affected by the *people* ingredient. People—specifically missionaries—were impacted by the four primary concepts of partnership practice. For example, *relationships* and *financial issues* impacted member care and financial provision for the missionary. *Vision* and *ministry philosophy,* when not shared by the church and agency, resulted in increased conflicts for the missionary. However, when the people involved were agency and church leaders, the relationship between these people impacted how *vision, ministry philosophy* and *finances* were viewed. When church and agency leaders had a positive relationship, shared understanding and resonance of *vision* and *ministry philosophy* increased, which further increased the likelihood that financial issues were viewed as a positive aspect of the partnership.

The practice of partnership between the church and agency need not be nebulous if a relevant model can guide this aspect of missions ministry. While missions leaders accept that personal relationships are critical in the church-agency partnership, an attempt to improve an inter-organisational partnership by focusing only on personal relationships is naively simplistic. Defining the church-agency partnership as revolving around the ingredients of *people, relationships, vision, ministry philosophy* and *finances* provides a targeted approach focusing on these elements to most effectively improve ministry practice. Improving these areas of church-agency partnership will be more effective than a vague approach to strengthen the relationship.

PARTNERSHIP IN MISSIONARY MOBILISATION

One of the factors that formed the background of this research study was a strong conviction of the importance of missionary mobilisation held by the leadership of Woodlands EFC. Our church had placed significant effort on developing awareness of missions in the congregation, identifying missionary candidates and investing in our partnership with missions agencies.

Exposure and Identification Phase Lacking Partnership

However, the research uncovered that very little partnership existed in the exposure and identification phase of mobilisation, though much more effort was placed on the formal candidature and sending part of mobilisation. In other words, the church would conduct its own screening process and, typically, only when the person was confirmed would the potential missionary begin candidating with the missions agency. The church had put in place its own mobilisation initiatives and tended to rely solely on its own criteria rather than a partnership with the agency in the exposure and identification phase. This practice continued despite the fact that Woodlands EFC had sent missionaries through a longstanding and positive relationship with these agencies, and was aware of its own lack of resources in identifying and screening potential missionaries.

The exposure and identification phase is defined as the earlier period when missions awareness and education in the congregation is developed, potential missionary candidates are identified and screened, and calling is discerned with other believers. This phase is differentiated from the later candidature and sending phase when the church, agency and missionary have already confirmed the calling, the person is officially a missionary candidate, application forms are completed, and the mechanisms for sending are discussed.

The observation that church-agency partnerships were not active in this earlier period of mobilisation was supported by the experiences of missionaries. Missionaries shared their own journeys, including numerous stories of how churches and missions agencies helped them separately, but not in partnership. For example, missionaries talked about receiving exposure to and a heart for missions that were cultivated within the local church. The testimonies and challenges by missionaries and missions leaders were significantly influential, but these accounts did not include a sense of partnership between the church and agency, such as coordination between the pastor and the missions agency. At most, a missionary from an agency would speak at a church event; while this was helpful, no sense of a partnership existed between the local church and missions agency.

One notable exception existed with regard to the lack of church-agency partnership in the exposure and identification phase of mobilisation. This exceptional case occurred when a missionary on the field lost his support from another church. The missions agency approached Woodlands EFC with the possibility that the missionary be sent from our church, because the agency director knew that the church had strong commitments to that mission field. A two-year process resulted in the missionary becoming a member of Woodlands EFC and subsequently being sent to the field.

In this case, a high level of cooperation between the church and agency was practised during the observation, confirmation, candidature and sending phase of the missionary. All parties gave highly positive feedback about this process. The factors that made this mobilisation example possible were pre-existing personal relationships between the church and agency, with high levels of trust and a strong alignment of vision and ministry philosophy for the particular mission field in question. Thus, all five primary concepts of people, relationships, vision, ministry philosophy and finances were strongly present and aligned in this exceptional case.

Candidature and Sending Phase had Stronger Partnership

Partnership was much stronger in the candidature and sending phase as compared to the exposure and identification phase. In this later phase, vision, ministry philosophy and finances were all tangible factors in the partnership. Two of our missionaries, one couple and one single, had past experiences in churches that did not want to work with a particular missions agency due, to misaligned vision and ministry philosophy. In both cases, this resulted in the missionaries eventually leaving the church and joining Woodlands EFC, where the vision was in alignment with that of both the missions agency and missionary. For these missionaries, the willingness of the church leaders to work with them, as well as the commonality of vision and ministry philosophy between the church and missions agency, was essential for their mobilisation. These ingredients were absent from their prior experiences with other churches and missions agencies.

Woodlands EFC sent one missionary couple twenty years earlier, at a time when the church was much smaller and did not have a missions pastor. In the case of this couple, commonality of vision and a willingness to send existed, but the church was just beginning to grapple with its role in missions, and the partnership with the agency was thus not strong. The missionary couple felt supported by the church and the agency separately, but shared that there was no relationship between the church and agency leaders, "I wouldn't say a strong partnership [existed]. I think we were the middlemen." For almost the entire candidature and sending process, communication between the church and agency occurred through the missionaries themselves, rather than between the leaders of the two organisations. The missionaries shared that this changed over time, when the church grew in its experience on how to engage in missions, especially when it appointed a missions pastor whose role was to communicate with the missions agencies. At this point, they felt the church-agency partnership grew stronger and they benefited from the increased communication.

This gap of partnership in the earlier phase of mobilisation is a potential area for growth. Missions-minded churches often have a passion for mobilising more missionaries. Woodlands EFC had programmes in place, regular challenges to the congregation, and intentionality to identify and develop candidates. However, the church still lacked many resources for this endeavour, such as mentors with missions experience and proven screening procedures for candidates. A missions agency often has these resources, but lacks access to a wide pool of committed Christians and the history of relationship that church leaders often have with a candidate.

Potential for Greater Mobilisation

Therefore, partnership between a local church and missions agency to identify potential missionaries and evaluate their suitability during the exposure and identification phase of mobilisation has good potential for long-term results. For this to take place, the five primary concepts of partnership must be in alignment between the church and agency. Strong relationships between leaders will increase understanding and alignment of vision and ministry philosophy, resolving concerns over finances and people.

MEMBER CARE ROLES FOR CHURCH & AGENCY

The provision of member care for missionaries is one of the crucial support functions of both the local church and missions agency. While missionaries generally appreciate all forms of member care, the study sought to determine, via interviews with the missionaries themselves, how the member care efforts of Woodlands EFC and the three missions agencies compared with what they valued the most. Common themes emerged from the responses of missionaries regarding the types of member care they appreciated more from the church and from the agency.

When missionaries were asked why they thought their responses were all similar despite their differing personalities and missions agencies, one missionary responded with an analogy of someone who goes to the office daily and returns home to his family in the evening.

He shared that for him, the church was like his family at home, while the agency helped him with his ministry in the workplace.

Member Care Valued *Most* by Missionaries

FROM CHURCH "FAMILY AT HOME"	FROM AGENCY "FAMILY AT WORK"	CHURCH & AGENCY TOGETHER
PRAYER	HEALTH CARE	MEMBER DEVELOPMENT
PASTORAL CARE	FIELD ENTRY	
PARENTAL/FAMILY CARE	MINISTRY FEEDBACK	MINISTRY REPORTS
RE-ENTRY TO HOME	MINISTRY STRATEGY	CHURCH/AGENCY POLICIES
MOBILISING THE CHURCH		HOME ASSIGNMENTS
FUNDRAISING STRUCTURES	CONFLICT RESOLUTION	FIELD VISITS

A missionary spends more hours each day on the field in his "workplace", and he needs member care that is relevant to the challenges he faces there. Fewer hours are spent on home assignment with the church, but this time is also critical, as the care provided by the church environment can be likened to that of a family at home.

Church: The Family at Home

When asked what was most valuable to them, the member care areas that missionaries talked about most frequently and valued more from the church were prayer, pastoral care, family, mobilisation of the church, re-entry to the home country and fundraising structures.

Prayer was a key way for missionaries to know that people cared for them and wanted to be involved in their work. Missionaries appreciated the prayer that their agency organised, but talked at greater length about prayer that their church organised. Sending prayer pointers was a helpful but limited avenue for member care, because they did not know whether people prayed or not. Aspects of member care they rated highly were hearing that groups gathered to pray for them and their ministry, knowing that the church was educating people on prayer for missions, and having specific people communicate with them about their prayer needs.

One missionary commented on the time when one monthly church prayer meeting was dedicated to missions and where missionaries from various countries joined in via video-conferencing. "It was just amazing to participate with the church because I felt that though I'm away, I'm participating and praying for missions. When I see others praying for our work, too, it's like 'wow'! That is a different kind of member care, which an agency would probably do quite differently." Another missionary said, "The church is more like a family." The difference in the care felt between the agency and church appeared to be due to the fact that agency prayer consisted of people in a specialist organisation, while the church was a larger family mobilising ordinary people to pray.

Similarly, pastoral care was a form of member care frequently mentioned as highly valuable and preferably received from the church. Agencies often provided these services, but missionaries cited more examples from the church. Small acts from the church, such as birthday gifts for missionaries' children, congratulations on an anniversary or

Christmas care packs, were greatly appreciated. "I don't feel that I'm alone. I feel like I have the whole church behind me," said one missionary.

Family is an extremely important member care issue in the Asian cultural context, especially concerning the aged parents of missionaries. Some agencies sent their staff to visit the parents of missionaries on important occasions such as Chinese New Year, and organised events such as dinner for them. Though the missionaries greatly appreciated these efforts, they spoke more about the impact that church visitations had on their family members. "It's the feeling of family in Woodlands EFC," said one missionary. Another commented on the difference between the efforts of the church and agency to connect with their family, "Even our extended family feels that, too. They sense it, so that's something that the agency can't do... It's just very formal. But the home church is different—very warm." Once again, given similar pastoral care from the church and agency, missionaries appreciated the care extended from the church because it felt more informal and more like family.

While the largest agency had structured some of these forms of family and pastoral care into their member care approach, all agency leaders concurred that the agency staff were not typically able to provide this type of care, as a small number of home staff would have many missionaries on the field. This is unlike the church, which has a longer history with the missionary and many more church members who could extend this care. In addition, the rate of turnover of members in a church is typically lower than that of staff in the home office of an agency, thus fostering a sense of permanence and longer-term relationship with the church. An agency leader commented that not all churches provide this type of member care for their missionaries, though he wished otherwise. One missionary suggested that the missions pastor or missions committee of a church must not feel that member care is solely their responsibility. Instead, they must be "challenging others to do the work rather than taking upon themselves all the responsibility of caring." He continued, "I think that is a key thing—the missions committee or the missions pastor being able to mobilise the people, whether in small groups or as individuals, to take care of missionaries." This current reality—that a significant amount of member care came from ordinary members of the congregation rather than officially from the missions committee—further enhanced the sense of informal family that missionaries experienced from Woodlands EFC.

Missionaries also talked about mobilisation as an aspect of member care they valued from the church. They felt cared for when the church educated the congregation about the missionary's ministry and what to pray for, sent teams to visit them, planned for future ministry and sought to raise more missionaries. Mobilisation of the church by leaders of the church was described as both raising more missionaries from within the congregation and engaging the wider church to be involved in their ministry through initiatives such as prayer, education and short-term mission trips. This differed from mobilisation from the missions agency perspective, which agency leaders described primarily as the first aspect—raising more missionaries to be sent to the field.

Re-entry to the home country was another form of member care from the church that was highly valued by missionaries. While the missions agency educated missionaries on re-entry issues and debriefed them upon re-entry, the church provided complementary relationships, where they experienced understanding and care when faced with re-entry challenges. "The care that was given the moment I touched down in Singapore was comprehensive and well thought through," said one missionary. "My broken leg didn't make my situation any better, but I thank God that there were church members who came forward to provide for every need I had: going to the hospital, going to the supermarket and bringing groceries to my house, because I was on crutches." Even when the church did not provide member care as well as it could have upon re-entry, missionaries stated that the church, rather than the missions agency, had great potential for re-entry care. Thus, missionaries' most acute needs upon re-entry are best met by member care provided through relationships within their sending church.

The way the local church raised funds for missionaries was frequently mentioned as an aspect of member care that they highly valued. The missionaries felt cared for not only by the individuals who supported them, but also by the fundraising structure of the sending church. In Woodlands EFC, the missions pastor leads the annual fundraising appeal to church members on behalf of the missionary. The financial needs of all missionaries are largely met within the local church, without the missionary having to canvas for support. One missionary recalled when he was first sent to the field, "I hear of missionaries who have to go around looking for financial support. I didn't have to do that at all." Another missionary related a similar appreciation, "We don't have to worry that this is the time of year when we need to come up with a speech or an appeal. Fundraising was fully handled by the committee and the missions pastor. That, to us, is something very, very encouraging. I think it's one of the beautiful things about our church. Everyone looks at our church just in awe of what the Lord has been doing, you know, in terms of the church being behind us." Thus, the fundraising structures were practised in such a way that the missionaries highly valued them as a form of member care.

Missions Agency: The Family at Work

Common themes also emerged regarding what missionaries valued from their missions agency. Responses across different missionaries were consistent with regard to their opinion that the following member care services should be provided by the agency and not the church: health care, field-entry, ministry and relational conflict issues. All these services were rendered because of matters that arose on the field. Thus, member care was most appreciated from the agency when it was extended for field matters.

The area of health care for emotional and physical well-being was a recurring member care issue among missionaries with regard to their agency. For missionaries in agencies that did not provide this, it was desired that the agency provide more of these services. In these cases, the requests were for basic medical services, such as referrals to trusted doctors or clinics on the field. Other missionaries were sent through agencies that provided medical services because they were viewed as an essential part of member care. These missionaries highly valued services such as having doctors and counsellors available to consult with on the field, as well as receiving regular debriefings on physical and emotional well-being. One missionary related that he was "very impressed by that in the agency; they really care for our whole well-being, the entire person." He was referring to the specialised support of medical doctors, counsellors and psychologists that was available, and felt that the church could never provide this type of support. While the church provided spiritual support and people who cared for him in personal relationships, the agency provided complementary expertise at a different level.

The period of first entry to the field was a crucial time for missionaries to receive member care. For some, this provision came in the form of pre-field cross-cultural training, which was separate from their theological training. Other missionaries shared stories about how the agency helped them get started with their new life. Commending the strong member care provided on the field, one missionary recalled how this was particularly helpful for new missionaries, "They go straight up to the language centre, so everything is in a sense provided for—housing, even furniture, when they first come. You appreciate that when you are new." Whether receiving language or logistics support, a missionary's first entry to the mission field is a critical period for them to receive member care from sending agencies and one they will continue to remember as something highly valuable.

Missionaries invested significant time discussing ministry issues as a major member care area valued from the agency. These services revolved around ministry issues, ranging from resolving conflict with team members and locals in the field to ministry feedback and being guided in ministry strategy. Coming from a missions agency with more resources, one missionary shared about how this empowered him, "The agency makes me feel that I can do much, much more. It's not just my field. In terms of mobilisation, networking and connecting with different countries, that kind of empowerment is fantastic."

Missionaries sent through agencies that were struggling to provide field structures talked about how they desired feedback and development in their ministry. One missionary wished that the agency would provide more guidance on ministry reports and evaluations, and judiciously share these results with Woodlands EFC, "I think that would be good because the church would know what I'm doing. And through that, the church can then look at it and see what type of training I need. Nobody did this for me."

All missionaries wanted to do well in their ministry and desired to receive member care that would help them perform well in the field. However, they were cautious about the church directing their field ministry because the church would not be aware of the field context. Instead, they preferred the agency to provide this kind of feedback and to inform the church. Said one missionary, "In that way, [the agency] can work with the church to see how to develop this worker." For member care related to ministry problems, especially relational conflicts on the field, missionaries were thankful for the care the agencies provided, such as leaders who gave oversight and helped to resolve matters, and counselling services that were made available. Overall, missionaries most valued member care from the agency when it was related to the work of ministry on the field.

Church and Missions Agency Caring in Partnership

When asked specifically about member care needs that can best be provided in partnership between their sending church and missions agency, missionaries had difficulty responding immediately. Some could not think of a response, while others did not feel the need to think about receiving more in the future, "In terms of member care, we are just very appreciative of what has been done." Others showed caution, stating that if partnership delved into field ministry strategy, then "the missionaries won't like that because it's out on the field that we do the work." Although missionaries wanted the church involved in their ministries, they were not in favour of additional meetings between the church and agency that would result in the sending church dictating the missionary's ministry from afar.

With that caution noted, missionaries still desired more communication between their church and agency regarding issues such as member development, ministry reports, policies and home assignments. During the focus group, missionaries who were in agencies that provided member development shared that they greatly appreciated how this enhanced their ministry. Language training, conferences, seminars and feedback regarding their ministry were all highly appreciated.

However, furthering of academic qualifications, formal study or time away from the field were development issues that missionaries often sensed a reluctance from the missions agency to support them. They felt that the agency leaders' reluctance was due to time away from the field and increased financial costs. Missionaries believed that this area would benefit from intentional partnership with the church. The agency would provide input regarding the impact of such studies on a missionary's field ministry, while the church would sense whether further study would contribute to the person as a whole, and provide necessary financial resources if approval was granted. One missionary highlighted how such a process had greatly encouraged him. Approval and funding were provided for him to pursue a master's degree due to structures within the agency, which gave him space to think about his ministry development, and the subsequent willingness of the church leaders to support this endeavour.

Ministry reports were another issue discussed by the focus group, concluding with full agreement by the missionaries that their agency should provide reports on the missionaries and their ministry, and share them with the church. Missionaries wanted the agency to provide feedback on their field ministry and communicate with the church, so that their church could know how to help them grow further. This reporting feedback was closely related to member development. One missionary shared that, though Woodlands EFC did not currently require such reports, he would not be surprised if the church chose to ask for them. Others thought that the agency was often reticent to share reports that may cast their missionaries in a negative light. Some missionaries were in agencies that required such reports, while others did not have reports written about them or their ministry. None of the agencies shared written reports with Woodlands EFC. Agency leaders who communicated more with the church preferred verbal updates to written reports.

Regarding policies set by the church and agency, missionaries did not want to be caught in the middle, having to explain and defend changes between their church and agency. They desired their church leaders and agency leaders to be in communication. For example, they wanted to know that their church was aware of important policy changes that their agency had made, so that they did not have to explain the rationale to their church leaders. In one scenario regarding a change in financial policy, the missionary had this exact concern even though the agency and church had communicated about the policy change. In this case, even though leaders from the agency and church were in dialogue, the missionary was not aware that this understanding had been reached, thus causing him concern.

Many missionaries talked about times when this kind of communication did not happen in the partnership. A recurring reason was the lack of a person in this leadership role. This occurred when no person in the church liaised with the agency, or when the agency faced a manpower shortage and lacked someone to connect with the church. In contrast, missionaries talked about the times when a missions pastor began visiting them or an agency leader began visiting the field and communicating with the church as an important milestone, where they sensed greater partnership between their church and missions agency. Having the right person in the appropriate leadership position to build the partnership between the church and agency was essential in helping the missionary experience optimal member care. Home assignment was one area where such communication between the church and agency was imperative. Missionaries desired their church and agency to work with each other to come to a common agreement on the frequency, length, purpose and schedule of home assignments.

Missionaries also shared about receiving field visits from both church and agency leaders as a welcome form of member care. Not only did personal visits on the field communicate interest in their ministry, it also allowed the sending church and home base of the missions agency to understand their field context. Missionaries shared that when Woodlands EFC first appointed a missions pastor who visited them on the field, that was the time when member care from the church significantly increased. They thought this improvement arose because the pastor brought his experiences back to the home church and mobilised the congregation to support the missionaries' ministry. Agency directors shared their desire to communicate more with pastors regarding such field visits, so that member care and information can be shared between the church and agency.

SUMMARY OF PARTNERSHIP FINDINGS

This description presents the preferred situation that occurs when the sending church is actively involved in member care. Ideally, the church provides this foundation of family-type member care by taking up member care services, such as parental care, pastoral care, prayer and re-entry to the home country. If the sending church does not engage in member care, the agency must increase its involvement and provide family-type care for the missionary. While such efforts from the missions agency would always be appreciated by any missionary, they are especially crucial for missionaries who do not receive family-type member care from their sending church. Fellow missionaries whose sending church did not engage in member care would talk about the agency family because they lacked this sense of family from their sending church, and pastoral care from the agency filled this critical need.

The reason some churches are not involved in member care could be due to a lack of knowledge that the local church should be involved in member care and the huge difference this makes to the well-being of the missionary, and not because of a lack of care on the part of the church. The agency could encourage the sending church to take up these roles, assuring them that the church would be far more effective providing these services as compared to the agency. This reinforcement could be empowering for many churches that think they cannot effectively contribute because they do not have the expertise of the missions agency.

When the agency knows that the church is taking care of the "family at home" type of member care, it can then effectively focus on the "family at work" aspect of the agency-missionary relationship. Missionaries shared that while they highly valued the missions agency family, they also recognised the difference between the church family and agency, as they were members of the agency in order to engage in the work of ministry. Thus, they felt most cared for when the agency family supported them in the work of ministry and the church family extended pastoral care while they were engaging in this ministry.

The distinction—church: the family at home and agency: the family at work—guides our practice by suggesting that the church and agency partner best when each organisation focuses on its respective domains. For example, the church should defer work issues to the agency and concentrate on areas in the family domain. Similarly, agencies should focus first on member care in relation to the work of ministry. Limited agency resources should go first to the work domain of the agency-missionary relationship.

chapter 4

THE RELATIONAL MODEL OF CHURCH-AGENCY PARTNERSHIPS

Ivan Liew

Thus far in the research findings, we have uncovered the key ingredients of church-agency partnership and insights regarding mobilisation and member care (Chapter 3). We also examined four partnership values that provide us with a biblical and theological grounding for how we should conduct our church-agency relationship (Chapter 2).

In this chapter, we will diagram these study findings one step at a time, thereby building the *Relational Model of Church-Agency Partnerships (REMCAP)*. The end result of *REMCAP* is a distillation of how the various elements of a church-agency partnership interact with one another and a description of how missionary mobilisation and member care occurs in church-agency partnerships. The model will, therefore, help us understand how our church-agency partnerships can be managed and guide us toward good practices.

PEOPLE, RELATIONSHIPS, VISION, MINISTRY PHILOSOPHY & FINANCES

The five key ingredients of a church-agency partnership are placed in a diagram to depict the connections between the ingredients that arose in the research study, thus providing greater insights into the findings. In Figure 1, the three outer circles represent the three key people in a church-agency sending partnership: the missions pastor, the agency director and the missionary being sent in partnership. The ring represents the relationship among these three people.

Figure 1. The Five Ingredients of a Church-Agency Partnership

The particular title of the agency leader may differ, and in some churches without a missions pastor, the missions chairman or senior pastor may be the person responsible for interfacing with the missions agency. Whatever the title may be, the particular person in the church and the corresponding person in the agency are both responsible for the church-agency partnership. Therefore, their personal and professional relationship is represented by the portion of the ring that connects them.

If one of these leaders from either the church or agency is not available for whatever reason, the church-agency partnership breaks down because there is no relationship. If the relationship is not positive due to earlier tensions, perceived lack of competency or frustrations with either organisation, then this negatively impacts the rest of the partnership. The upper "impact arrow" in Figure 1 depicts the fact that relationship between the church and agency leader impacts how vision, ministry philosophy and finances are viewed and practised in the partnership. If the relationship is viewed positively, then vision, ministry philosophy and finances are also viewed positively. The level to which these three ingredients are shared and mutually understood is used as a measure for evaluating the church-agency partnership, which in turn impacts the missionary, as depicted by the lower "impact arrow."

When a missionary does not have a primary sending church but raises funds from a wide variety of sources, there is often no clarity with regard to who the sending church is. In such a situation, there can be no church-agency partnership in practice, and the missionary receives suboptimal member care. When a sending church exists but does not identify a missions leader as the person responsible for communicating with the agency, the church-agency relationship is severely handicapped and the missionary still receives suboptimal member care.

Therefore, REMCAP recommends that missionaries have one primary sending church and one person in the church whose responsibility is to partner with the missions agency. This clarity almost always exists on the missions agency's part, but is sometimes absent on the church side of the relationship. In the original research study, agency directors discussed the difficulties they faced when this clarity did not exist. They compared this to the highly favourable situation where churches were clear about their sending role. In Singapore, the church at which a missionary is a member usually considers itself the primary sending church. Even when other churches or individuals outside the primary sending church contribute financially to the missionary, clarity still exists regarding the primary sending church.

Woodlands Evangelical Free Church has always been clear about its role as the sending church, even when, as a small church, it sent its first missionaries in the 1980s. However, the identification of the particular person in the church responsible for missions and partnerships with missions agencies was not well defined in the early years. Since 1995 the church has increasingly realised the importance of having a missions pastor who holds this responsibility. One missionary shared about his early mobilisation experiences when the church lacked this clarity:

> Because there was no missions pastor, we were the middlemen to negotiate between the church and the agency whenever things were needed, or regarding where to go and all those things. In those days, we had to be pioneers in mobilising ourselves.

The same missionary also described how much better things were when someone actively took up the role to communicate with the missions agency.

While it is common in Singapore for a missionary's home church to provide a large percentage of the financial support and take on the role as the primary sending church, this is the exception rather than the rule in other sending nations such as the United States. *REMCAP* suggests that, even if a local church is unable to provide a significant percentage of their missionaries' financial support, the home church should still consider taking up the "family at home" role in missionary care, acknowledge their biblically central role in missionary sending, and identify a person responsible for the agency partnership. In a large church, this may be the missions pastor, whereas in other cases, it may be the senior pastor or a lay missions chairman.

In summary, although it is true to say that people and relationships are important in the church-agency partnership, such a statement is too general. Instead, it would be clearer to say there are three types of relationships at work. First, the relationship between the missions pastor and agency director is absolutely critical in the church-agency partnership. This relationship is both personal and professional, for there must be trust in each other's character and competence for a healthy inter-organisational relationship. The second is the relationship between the missionaries and their church, and the third is the relationship between the missionaries and their missions agency. These relationships, which can be considered vehicles through which mobilisation and member care occur, will be discussed later in this chapter.

THE CHURCH-AGENCY RELATIONSHIP

The *Relational Model for Church-Agency Partnerships* seeks to further describe the crucial relationship between the missions pastor and agency director. Many leaders intuitively know that investment in this relationship is valuable and "meeting up for coffee" is helpful, but this can lose its purpose without more specific guidance.

The biblical, theological and historical foundations help us at this point. The values derived from Trinitarian theological and historical effectiveness can and should guide the church-agency relationship. *REMCAP* proposes four partnership values that guide the church and agency: (1) biblical centrality of the church, (2) equal value of church and agency in missions, (3) glad submission and mutual deference, and (4) joyful fellowship and encouragement (see Figure 2).[8]

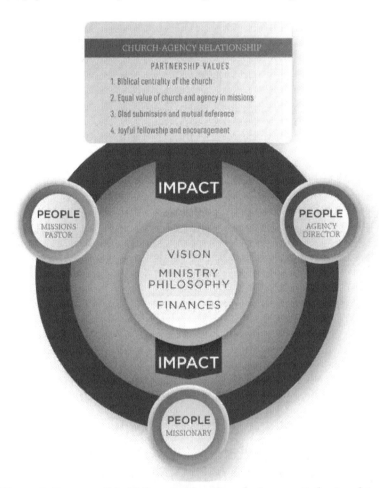

Figure 2. Partnership Values in the Church-Agency Relationship

With these partnership values in place, we can build on the earlier statement that the church-agency relationship impacts the important alignment of vision, ministry philosophy and finances. Now we can more specifically state that clarifying and aligning our personal and organisational values to these four partnership values will, in turn, positively impact how the key ingredients of partnership are aligned.

Missions pastors and agency directors typically agree that strengthening their relationship is important, but why we should do so and how to do it are often vague and undefined. While improving personal relationships and having informal gatherings certainly help the relationship, the presumption that these efforts alone will improve the overall church-agency partnership is naïve and idealistic. Without concrete guidance regarding what to do and the reasons for such a strategy's effectiveness, this important relational investment becomes so vague that it is usually neglected amidst the reality of competing demands on the leaders' time.

The *Relational Model for Church-Agency Partnerships* provides this needed clarity for church-agency relationship. The partnership values serve as a powerful guide and motivator due to their strong biblical and theological foundations. *REMCAP* recommends that agency directors and missions pastors discuss these four values together, thus laying a foundation for shared values. At the start of a new partnership, some leaders may find it helpful to include these values into a memorandum of understanding. For those with an already existing partnership, the very process of dialogue and building shared understanding strengthens the partnership relationship.

For example, when discussing what the biblical centrality of the church means, the agency director and missions pastor will voice their opinions on the biblical basis of the agency as compared with the local church, a topic that is likely to have never been discussed personally between the two leaders even though it is a foundational matter. The discussion can then proceed to affirming the equal value of both organisations with respect to the task of missions. Valuing one another would involve understanding and respecting the partner organisation's objectives and contributions. Such discussions increase trust in the other party and greatly improve relationships.

In this manner, discussion on partnership values helps to deepen trust in relationship far beyond the first coffee discussion and superficial topics. When missions pastors and agency leaders talk about the partnership values in *REMCAP*, they begin by sharing the foundational *why* of partnership and proceed to discuss the *how* when they talk about the key ingredients of people, relationships, vision, ministry philosophy and finances.

The process of discussing the partnership values, the scriptural basis for each value and what each value means for our own organisation brings tremendous strengthening of partnership between the church and missions agency. I have experienced this truth multiple times, both in the course of this research when I discussed the model with agency directors who were part of the original study and when I shared these values with others in the lead-up to the publication of this book. Shared values strengthen partnerships, especially when these partnership values guide our relationships and are rooted in biblical and theological truths.

MOBILISATION & MEMBER CARE AS RELATIONSHIP

The original study aimed to determine the partnership practices that optimise missionary mobilisation and member care—elements that have not yet been inserted into the diagram. An important realisation

I came to when analysing the data was that mobilisation and member care could be understood as occurring through relationships with both the church and missions agency. More specifically, the church-missionary and agency-missionary relationships facilitate mobilisation in the early stage of sending the missionary to the field and member care in the later stage when the missionary is serving on the field.

During the interviews, both the missionaries and directors spent significant time sharing about the relationships among the church, agency and missionary. Missionaries consistently talked about the member care services they appreciated coming from the agency and those that they valued coming from the church. This difference in member care was validated by the agency directors and listed in the *REMCAP* model under either the church or the agency (see Figure 3 on the following page). After the research study was completed, the model underwent several rounds of discussions with leaders from various churches and agencies, and we felt that this distinction in member care was best captured by the phrases, "church family at home" and "agency family at work." In this analogy, the missions agency is best suited to meet member care needs related to the work of ministry on the field, while the church is best suited to care for the missionary the way family members at home do when a loved one leaves the home for work.

Certain matters in mobilisation and member care are not optimally addressed by only one organisation. While church-agency coordination is not needed for every matter, certain issues require input from both organisations, and these are listed in *REMCAP* in a separate box indicating "church-agency-missionary communication" required.

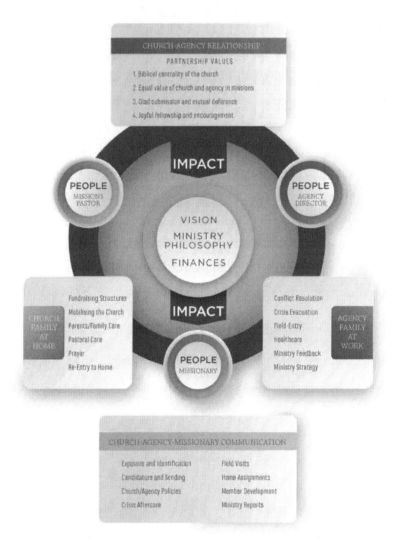

Figure 3. The Relational Model of Church-Agency Partnerships

SUMMARY OF *REMCAP*

After having integrated multiple parts of the research study one at a time, we have now arrived at *REMCAP*. At the conclusion of this chapter, a summary overview of the model would help the reader grasp *REMCAP* in its entirety.

The church-agency partnership consists of five key ingredients of people, relationships, vision, ministry philosophy and finances. The missions pastor and agency director (or similar positions) are the key people responsible for the inter-organisational relationship. The partnership values of this relationship should be founded on: (1) biblical centrality of the church, (2) equal value of church and agency in missions, (3) glad submission and mutual deference, and (4) joyful fellowship and encouragement.

The quality of the partnering relationship between the missions pastor and agency director impacts how vision, ministry philosophy and finances are viewed between the organisations. In turn, how these ingredients are exercised impacts the mobilisation and member care experience of the missionary.

Good practice of partnership includes both the church and agency being involved in the missionary's life and ministry. Certain areas in mobilisation and member care are most effective when addressed by the church, while others are most valued by the missionary when they are addressed by the missions agency. The distinction between these can be summarised as "church family at home" and "agency family at work." Some areas of mobilisation and member care do not fall into either category and are best practised by the church and agency together, thus requiring greater inter-organisational communication.

APPLYING & IMPROVING THE PARTNERSHIP MODEL

With the model published and the research study completed, the next question was whether it would be applicable to a wider group in Singapore. Every research study has its limitations, and mine was that it was a narrow case study of one church and three missions agencies. While the study was deep, it was not wide enough.

Would leaders from other churches and missions agencies consider the findings and model helpful as they deal with varying opinions, financial struggles and crises on the field?

As I began to share the research, a small group of leaders from churches and missions agencies responded with a willingness to apply the model and help me take it further. Not only did they learn about the research findings and *REMCAP*, we began to meet together to apply the principles to our own partnership relationships between the churches and agencies represented in the group. Their participation was the next stage of the research process.

We called ourselves Churches and Missions Agencies Together, or CMAT, and without these co-labourers, this book would not have been written. The next chapter describes who we are and what we did together to improve our own partnership practice.

chapter 5

A WORKING GROUP OF CHURCH & AGENCY LEADERS

Ivan Liew

In October 2014, a group of leaders from four churches and three missions agencies gathered to discuss the essential, but thorny issue of church and missions agency partnership in Singapore. Comprising mostly missions pastors, agency directors and member care specialists, this working group reviewed the research study findings and the *Relational Model of Church-Agency Partnerships (REMCAP)*. In light of the partnership values and model agreed upon, we analysed the case studies that each person brought to the meeting.

After the initial meeting, participants shared that these conversations were the most open and transparent exchanges we have ever had between church and missions agency leaders. We agreed to continue to meet four times a year, and a subset of this group became the steering committee that drafted strategic plans for subsequent gatherings. We clarified why we were investing this time with one another and what we hoped to achieve through it.

This chapter talks about how we started and how this process benefited us, in hopes that you, as a church or missions agency leader, can envision yourself as part of such a group that openly discusses the issues and questions church and agency leaders are all thinking about, but have never brought into the open. We share who we are and what we have done, and hope that others will likewise recognise the need for church-agency partnerships and resonate with the partnership values the working group has agreed upon.

If you and the organisation you lead think in like-minded ways, then the statements and values expressed in this chapter will be extremely helpful, both in providing much-needed clarity at the start of new partnerships and strengthening existing partnerships.

WHO IS CMAT

We, Churches and Missions Agencies Together (CMAT), are a working group of missions leaders of churches and missions organisations in Singapore who expectantly recognise that partnerships between local churches and missions agencies have immense potential to advance world evangelisation.[9] We are committed to church-agency partnerships that reflect the image of Trinitarian relationships, incubate effective missions practice and nurture optimal missionary care. At the same time, we admit that the effective practice of such inter-organisational relationships is, unfortunately, rare. We know that our own partnership practice falls short, and thus we seek to learn and work together within an environment of relational trust and transparency.

CMAT VALUES

We affirm four values of church-agency relationships that undergird our partnership practice. These values form the basis of *REMCAP*, which further describes our partnership practice: (1) biblical centrality of the church, (2) equal value of church and agency in missions, (3) mutual deference and glad submission, and (4) joyful fellowship and encouragement. We now present a summary of the biblical and theological bases for these values.

Note that the final paragraph under each value contains an explanation that summarises the biblical basis, and may serve as a standalone summary description. These values can be adopted by a church or missions agency and written into the policy document regarding the church-agency partnership. Written for both the church and missions agency, these values are shared and more helpful to partnership practice than a church and missions agency having separate partnership values.

Biblical Centrality of the Church

Christ established his *ekklesia* (Mt 16:18), which from New Testament times, has always had its expression as a local gathering of believers who adhered to the creed "Jesus is Lord" (1 Cor 12:3; Rom 10:9). When Jesus commissioned his eleven remaining disciples to "go and make disciples of all nations", this command was therefore given to a localised group of his *ekklesia*. When God called Paul and Barnabas to missionary work, the Holy Spirit spoke to the church in Antioch, who commissioned and sent forth this missionary band (Acts 13:2-3). Thus, the local church was established first, and missionary bands— the functional precursor to missions agencies—were subsequently called out from the church.

We affirm the biblical centrality of the local church and the Lausanne Committee for World Evangelization's statement that for parachurch organisations, "independence of the church is bad, co-operation with the church is better, service as an arm of the church is best." The mandate of global missions was given first to the local church and subsequently to the missionary band. While the global Church is entrusted with the call to missions, the responsibility and ownership of missions rests primarily with the church and secondarily with the missions agency.

Equal Value of Church and Agency in Missions

While the church is given the first responsibility and ownership for global missions, missions agencies have a strong biblical and historical evidence for their existence and effectiveness. When Paul and Barnabas were sent by the church in Antioch (Acts 13:2-3), they functioned as an autonomous group while still consulting and involving the Antiochean church in major decisions and subsequent ministry (Acts 15:2, 22). Throughout church history, specialist groups such as missions societies, monastic orders and the New Testament missionary bands have had a much greater impact on world evangelisation than local churches or denominations. In post-Reformation times, the missions agency has similarly proved far more effective than the local church in missionary endeavours to unreached and least reached peoples.

This tension between the biblical centrality of the church and the greater effectiveness of the missions agency—evidenced historically and in Scripture through missionary bands—can be addressed by a Trinitarian model for partnership. Relationships between the Father, Son and Holy Spirit simultaneously evidence differing roles and the equal value of distinct persons within the Godhead (Jn 5:18, 8:19). Since we are created in the image of God, the Trinitarian *perichoresis*[10] provides us with the divine blueprint for our inter-personal and inter-organisational relationships.

We affirm the equal value of the church and agency in cross-cultural missions. In partnership, the church and missions agency should equally value each other, esteeming each other in mutual interdependence in the joint missions endeavour.

Glad Submission and Mutual Deference

Within the Trinity, equal value of one another perfectly co-exists with the differing roles of each person in the Godhead. Jesus gladly submits to the will of the Father who has given him a mission to complete (Mt 20:23; Lk 22:42; Jn 6:38). Jesus is able to accomplish this mission because the Father has deferred authority to the Son (Jn 10:17-18). This intertwining ministry extends to the Holy Spirit in John 16. Jesus ends his earthly ministry so that the Spirit can begin his ministry (v.7). Christ defers to the Holy Spirit, who accomplishes his work of continuing the ministry of the Son and glorifying him (vv.14-15), so the deference is mutual and the submission is glad.

The church has biblical centrality and therefore, the primary responsibility and ownership for missions, but the church will choose to defer authority over certain matters to the missionary band and missions agency (Acts 13). Deference in this manner flows out from the church that esteems the missions agency with equal value in missions. In turn, the missions agency serves the church in its missions involvement, including the sending of missionaries. Such is the expression of glad submission and biblical centrality of the church.

We affirm that glad submission and mutual deference will characterise our conduct and communication amidst the many decisions that will be made within our church and missions agency partnership.

Joyful Fellowship and Encouragement

Not only does the Trinitarian *perichoresis* provide us with the divine design for relationship, but Christ draws us into the triune relationship to participate in this joyful fellowship. We are invited to experience unparalleled love and unity with the Father, Son and Holy Spirit, and with one another, so that the world may believe that Jesus is Lord (Jn 17:20-26). Thus, we are created in the image of God to experience the joy of fellowship, which is inseparable from the work of missions.

Such practice of joyful fellowship and encouragement has not always been realised, whether in present times or the first century. However, Paul presents this as the biblically preferred model in his relationship as a missionary with the churches he planted and with those who supported him. The Ephesian church evidenced this close fellowship with Paul (Acts 20:36-38). Paul thanks the Philippians for their *koinonia* (Php 1:5), often translated as partnership, sharing and participation in the gospel. The pervasive sense of mutual relationship and encouragement throughout the Philippian epistle, together with Christ's prayer for inclusion in the joyful Trinitarian relationship of love (Jn 17:20-26), forms the biblical basis for joyful fellowship and encouragement in the church-agency relationship.

We affirm that joyful fellowship and encouragement between the church and missions agency is the biblical norm for our partnership relationship. This relational expression of unity in the body of Christ is crucially embodied in the personal relationship forged between our church and missions agency leaders, for their relationship sets the tone for the inter-organisational partnership.

CMAT RESEARCH PROCESS

When the first CMAT group began, we spent significant time discussing both the partnership values and how *REMCAP* worked.

We recommend that other groups of church and agency leaders take a similar approach up to this point. The process of discussing the values and meaning of the model greatly strengthened the existing partnerships and relationships among the first CMAT participants. In addition, the first CMAT group improved on *REMCAP* and developed good practice guidelines with which all members agreed.

Validation and Improvement

The original research results and *REMCAP* were improved upon by extensive discussions within CMAT. While the participants agreed with the research and model, they had differing opinions regarding two phrases, which they clarified and eventually changed.

First, one of the partnership values was rephrased from "biblical primacy of the church" to "biblical centrality of the church". We agreed that the original phrasing carried a connotation of superiority, which was not helpful. After much discussion on the meaning of different terms, one member suggested "biblical centrality", which we all agreed, was an improved form.

A second change to the original model was a rephrasing of the distinction of "church family at home" and "agency family at work". Even before the start of the group, feedback had been received that the original term "church is family; agency is work" communicated a truthful distinction, but could give the wrong connotation that the missions agency is overwhelmingly corporate or work focussed. Again, after much discussion and acknowledgement on the importance of the agency family, CMAT decided upon the terms, "church family at home" and "agency family at work", to communicate the distinction between the roles of the church and agency with regard to their missionary.

Good Practice Guidelines

Early in the formation of CMAT, we agreed to document good practice guidelines from every discussion. Not only would this foster a rigorous thought process and crystallise our mutual understanding into the written word, but it would also advance the church-agency partnership research. Further practical guidance would be drawn out from *REMCAP*. At first, these documents were written only for internal consumption. Later, we decided to write them in a book for wider distribution. Thus, Part 2 of this book contains the good practice guidelines for church-agency partnership issues that we felt were foundational.

In this manner, CMAT continued the research process, where the first findings of the church-agency relationships and the resultant model was further validated and improved by a wider group of church and agency leaders.[11] Good practice guidelines were formed and agreed upon by the churches and missions agencies represented.

Participants

The participants of CMAT comprised a mixture of missions pastors from local churches, as well as national directors and member care specialists from missions agencies. With four churches and three missions agencies represented, several missionary sending partnerships existed within the group itself. Thus, we were a working group with church-agency relationships in progress, who sought to not only discuss the matters but also produce good practice guidelines for ourselves and others.

CMAT was guided by a steering committee led by Ivan Liew (Woodlands Evangelical Free Church) with the following members: Jeffrey Lum (Bartley Christian Church), Belinda Ng (SIM, Serving in

Participants of the CMAT Pilot Working Group

CHURCHES	LEADERS
ADAM ROAD PRESBYTERIAN CHURCH	LER WEE MENG
	LIM LUCK YONG
AGAPE BAPTIST CHURCH	THOMAS LIM
BARTLEY CHRISTIAN CHURCH	JEFFREY LUM*
	SERENE LUM
WOODLANDS EVANGELICAL FREE CHURCH	IVAN LIEW*

MISSIONS AGENCIES	LEADERS
OMF SINGAPORE	DAPHNE TEO*
	PAUL TAN
PIONEERS INASIA	W M SYN
SIM, SINGAPORE	BELINDA NG*
	KELVIN CHEN
	LEONARD LEOW

CONSULTANT	
LINK CARE CENTER	BRENT LINDQUIST*

Steering committee members

Mission), and Daphne Teo (OMF, Overseas Missionary Fellowship). Brent Lindquist (President, Link Care Center, USA) served as a consultant to the working group and the development of this book. Not only did all the remaining participants shown in Table 2 contribute to the discussions and case studies in the working group, but they also contributed by authoring one of the chapters in Part 2 of this book.

As the first pilot working group, we sought to build trust and transparency, aiming for a depth of interaction that precluded us growing into a large group. Now that we have completed our objectives, we have ended our group meetings and are seeking to assist other church and missions agency leaders who wish to enter into a similar practice. The formation and collaboration of additional groups, with more churches and missions agencies involved, will further strengthen the model, widen the community, and result in jointly developed good practice guidelines that will benefit more missionaries, missions agencies and churches.

DISCUSSING CASE STUDIES

Exploring case studies together was an essential part of our group meetings and a key method of furthering the research process. This allowed for application of partnership values and *REMCAP* to real-world scenarios that the group faced. Such transparent discussion of case studies would not have been possible without trust and mutual respect for one another in an environment of joyful fellowship.

Members of the group wrote case studies and brought these to the group for discussion according to the following guidelines.

1. First, the purpose of the case study is to explore application of the partnership values and *REMCAP* to actual church-agency partnership practice. The purpose is achieved when exploration culminates in good practice guidelines that are agreed upon by members of the pilot working group, representing a range of churches and missions agencies.[12]

2. Second, the topic of the case study could be an actual incident or a composite of factual incidents and situations. The case

study should not identify particular individuals, but may identify organisations within the pilot working group when permission from the organisation's representative is granted. Discussing real situations, in the presence of representatives of those organisations, brings great depth and authenticity to the application of values and writing of good practice guidelines.

3. Third, the case study should be brief, comprising 100–250 words. This length includes two to four specific questions at the end of the case study that direct the ensuing discussion. The questions should highlight the specific topic at hand and draw out good church-agency partnership practice guidelines that the group seeks to agree upon.

Every case study was discussed transparently. Some cases were written from either a distinctly church or distinctively missions agency perspective. Others were particularly painful, and we noted the mistakes made on the part of church leaders, agency leaders and the missionaries themselves.

The questions and challenges in each case study were discussed with openness in light of our shared values and *REMCAP*. Our conclusions were documented and distributed in writing for amendments and agreement at the next quarterly meeting. In this manner, we engaged in decision-making in community and developed good practice guidelines endorsed by leaders from the variety of churches and agencies represented.

After 11 case studies were discussed and documented over the course of one year, we decided on the foundational topics that would form Part 2 of this book. Each chapter in this section uses one of these case studies to illuminate that particular topic. While the names of missionaries, organisations and locations have been changed, each story is a real case of church-agency partnership that had been personally encountered by members of CMAT.

We now present one of our case studies to illustrate the joint analysis by both church and missions agency leaders, and the mutually agreed upon good practice guidelines. It demonstrates the partnership values and *REMCAP* in practice, with practical guidance in a real-world scenario where black and white clarity may not exist. Like all case studies discussed and documented, the recommendations presented are jointly held by all CMAT members. The process of discussion was extremely helpful for the group, and we believe sharing them with others will be similarly helpful. However, we recognise that our analysis is far from exhaustive and our conclusions cannot be the answer to all such cases.

Church Involvement in Field Conflict

Andy and Evelyn were experienced missionaries serving in Japan in a multinational team of a missions agency. Inter-personal conflict and differences in ministry strategy arose within the team. Field leadership was aware, and various interventions and counselling sessions took place, but the conflict was not fully resolved over several years. Andy and Evelyn's sending church believed that it should not generally interfere in field matters, so their church leaders initially restricted their role to encouragement and pastoral care.

However, after two years the church leaders felt that their missionaries were not being fairly treated and became concerned for their emotional health. The church leaders shared their concerns with the agency director, with whom they had a good relationship, indicating that if significant changes could not be made for their missionaries within the agency, they would remove them from the agency even though they did not want to do so.

1. When should the church "step in" to field matters, if at all?

2. How should the agency involve the church when their missionaries are involved in a field conflict?

Group Analysis

Interpersonal conflict is always multifaceted, with each person having a role and part to play in the dispute. In such scenarios, dialogue should be tripartite at an early stage, involving the church, agency and missionary. If the church does not engage the agency but hears only from the missionary, then a one-sided view will emerge. While the sending church is right to have a strong interest in the well-being of its people, even with the best of intentions, they may not have the whole picture. Hence, a joint decision is always best. The solution is never as simple as removing the missionary and solving the problem.

Should the church ever step in to field matters? The group concurred that it should—after an appropriate time has passed. Stepping in too soon will cause more damage and be seen as inappropriate interference. For the agency, wisdom is needed regarding when to involve the church. Alerting the church to every problem is foolish, but the agency should also not delay communication to the church until the problem has become so serious that there is no choice but to communicate! By this time, the church would likely be aware that a problem exists and become frustrated that they have not been involved.

In this particular case, there existed a joint agreement between the church and agency that enough time had been given to attempt to resolve the conflict. Effort had been invested by all parties over a period of years—not months. While the church eventually approached the agency to request for significant changes to occur, this happened only after numerous tripartite discussions involving the church, agency and missionaries had taken place over a long period of time.

An important factor was that the missionaries also wanted significant change. When the church leaders approached the agency, making their feelings and position known, it was a risk to the relationship, for they did not know how the agency would respond. In the end, the director of the agency agreed with much of the church's concerns. Within the agency, there existed differing assessments of the conflict and the missionaries in question. However, the agency director concurred with the church and took appropriate action. As a result, the missionaries changed teams and are doing well in ministry, and the church-agency relationship became stronger.

The agency director emphasised the importance of a pre-existing tripartite relationship. In this case, the church, agency and missionaries all knew and trusted one another well. The director shared, "Be slow to take sides. It doesn't mean that everyone in my organisation is right. Our ultimate allegiance is to the Lord, not to my organisation."

Consultant Response

This case illustrates a common scenario with an uncommon ending, that is, things worked out well for the church-agency relationship. While not unique to Singapore, this case illustrates the strength that can come from tripartite relationships because of the closeness of the

Singaporean context. It may not be easy to develop this closeness in larger countries, but this would still be a worthy goal.

One concern that arises out of this is the long time it took for everyone to try to solve the problem. Is this an Asian distinctive of not wanting to confront? People may hold various opinions, but the presence of a working document that clearly outlines the process of working through the presenting difficulties would, no doubt, be of benefit in any culture. Knowing what to do, and when to do it, would be of great help regardless of our perspective regarding a particular behaviour in the conflict situation. Let's look at the first component of knowing what to do.

As it becomes apparent that there exist problems on the field between a missionary and the team, it is important to address the causal factors. Such factors could include work issues, personal traits, or most likely, a combination of both. In addition, the local context, whether cultural or with particular local believers, could form additional factors.

An initial step is to ask, "What are some of the issues causing this particular conflict?" The missions agency and the church can list their concerns, thus beginning the working document that alerts parties of the concerns. Each party is thus allowed to surface the concerns and various issues.

Once this question has been asked, the agency would determine whether an issue needed to be addressed. In the case of a missionary on the field, the agency has the responsibility to investigate. If deemed necessary, an action plan would be developed and applied, with appropriate timelines for review.

When these steps are taken, the question of "when to do it" often becomes evident in the investigation and action plan. If a problem is found, then the action plan decides on the "when", which is typically "now."

GOOD PRACTICES FOR PARTNERSHIP

We have reached the end of Part 1 of this book and have laid the theoretical foundation for church-agency partnerships. Having made it thus far, you the reader have an overview of the state of missions partnership in Singapore, the current research on church-agency partnerships and how a model for such partnerships was developed.

The *Relational Model for Church-Agency Partnerships* has been validated and is in use by CMAT, the working group that has furthered the research and jointly written this book. Each chapter in Part 2 of this book applies the research and model to a particular topic within church-agency partnerships that we consider foundational.

In our experience and discussions, we find these topics raised repeatedly in many sending scenarios. Therefore, we believe these are the most important topics to analyse first, as having good practice guidelines agreed upon by both the church and agency regarding these issues will result in tremendous dividends for our partnerships and for the missionaries sent through them.

part 2

GOOD PRACTICES FOR PARTNERSHIP

chapter 6

VISION & MINISTRY PHILOSOPHY
Ler Wee Meng & W M Syn

Over the years, Christ Community Church has grown a heart for ministry to Vietnamese people both in Singapore and abroad in short-term missions involvement. A couple from the church, Ben and Angela, had served in these outreach ministries, particularly to Vietnamese students, and subsequently responded to God's call to be long-term missionaries in Vietnam. They had the strong support of their church leaders, who were keen to see the student ministry started in Singapore take place in Vietnam. Thus began the partnership discussions with the home side of an agency called Global Mission.

While the church found Global Mission's mobilisation and field-based care structures complementary to the local church's efforts, some complications arose. Global Mission had contacted its field teams in the Vietnamese city that the church planned to send Ben and Angela knowing that the current missionaries there did not have a ministry to students. The existing Global Mission missionaries in Vietnam then entered the discussion. However, they reasoned that there was no need for a student ministry because local churches were already engaging in this area of ministry.

The discussion continued over a period of several months, but there was no progress. Though Christ Community Church was initially keen on sending Ben and Angela through Global Mission, it finally decided to withdraw their application from the agency. Ben and Angela continued to work with their church leaders, who subsequently direct-sent them to Vietnam.

WALKING IN AGREEMENT

Local churches and mission agencies have the potential to form mutually beneficial complementary partnerships. However, challenges arise when differences between the church and agency begin to surface. While differences are a natural part of any relationship, these often reveal a disconnect in vision, approach or ministry philosophy between the two organisations.

Without a common vision and ministry philosophy, the partnership journey will be fraught with obstacles. Such rocky relationships sometimes occur because partners assume they share the same vision and ministry philosophy due to on overly idealistic view that both parties desire to send a missionary to the field. For this reason, achieving mutual clarity about vision and ministry philosophy is essential at the start of the partnership, because differences are easier to work out at this point and the option exists to not begin the partnership in the first place.

Defining Vision and Ministry Philosophy

Partnership vision can be defined as what a local church, missions agency and missionary aim to achieve together. The greater the clarity and alignment of vision, the more likely it is for the partnership to be successful.

Ministry philosophy seeks to explain why a church or agency does what it does in the process of sending a missionary, to achieve its vision.

The key word is "why" an organisation does what it does; therefore, ministry philosophy is more related to an organisation's values rather than a chosen strategy. Values describe what is underlying and are of such importance that they are non-negotiable for an organisation as it works to achieve its vision. In contrast, strategy is the plans for how an organisation will achieve that vision, and it can and should change over time.

In summary, vision is "what" a church or agency seeks to achieve, and ministry philosophy is "why" this is important to the organisation. Successful partnerships require both parties to have alignment of vision and ministry philosophy.

Alignment does not equate to being exactly the same on all accounts, as no two organisations would have exactly the same vision or ministry philosophy. The comparison words, "same" and "common", do not refer to a facsimile replica, but alignment and commonality, particularly in the area of partnership. The best partnerships are complementary in nature. Thus, within the scope of the partnership to send a missionary to a particular mission field, a church and missions agency must have alignment of vision and ministry philosophy.

Excluding Strategy

One may question why "strategy" is not included in our list of requirements for alignment, and why this chapter is not titled "Vision, Ministry Philosophy and Strategy." This is not to say that strategy is not important. However, in the original research and pilot Churches and Missions Agencies Together (CMAT) group, strategy was seen as a secondary step that follows the establishment of common underlying ministry philosophy and values. The first reason is that strategy may be adjusted in the course of one or two years due to changes in the environment. Second, the *Relational Model of Church-Agency Partnerships (REMCAP)* specifies that strategy-related decision on the field should be made by field leaders of the missions agency and not the church; thus, the church practises the CMAT value of mutual deference even though it has biblical centrality in missions.

For example, a local church may have an underlying philosophy and value that emphasises productivity of its missionaries and expects certain results in the year. When this is not talked through, unreasonable expectations can be placed on the missionaries even before they have had time to learn the culture, grow in the language and develop quality relationships on the field.

Though strategy is not one of the five key ingredients of church-agency partnership in *REMCAP*, this does not mean that a church and missions agency should never discuss strategy. The more invested a church is on a field, the more missionaries it will send to that field, and the more money is given to projects, the more a church will desire to be involved in field strategy. In addition, a church may adopt a people group or invest in additional ministries that extend beyond the scope of the missionary and that particular missions agency. Such involvement furthers a church's knowledge of the field and its desire to be engaged in the strategy of its missionary's ministry.

Not every element of the church's missions vision will overlap with a mission agency's scope of work, as was the case with Ben and Angela. There may exist differences in field strategy and focus, or gaps in resourcing of the organisations. In such cases, the church and missions agency should discuss the preferred strategy and resources that each organisation brings to the partnership, deciding whether to work together or not.

The more a church wants to be involved in field strategy, the greater the field knowledge its leaders must have and the more closely aligned its preferred strategy must be with that of the missions agency. However, the final activities and strategy of the missionary must still be determined by field leaders of the missions agency and not the church.

BEGINNING A PARTNERSHIP

In Ben and Angela's case, they had already possessed some knowledge of the field and the language, and they had a particular vision in mind due to their involvement with the Vietnamese diaspora in Singapore. This level of engagement of the local church necessitated further discussion of not only vision and ministry philosophy, but also strategy.

Assess the Differences

As discussions between the church and agency proceeded, it became apparent that there existed significant differences in how each organisation viewed the ministry that Ben and Angela were to engage in—their vision was to grow a vibrant ministry among Vietnamese students on the field, just like they had in their home church. Unfortunately, this specific vision was not shared by the field leadership of the missions agency. They could not fit student ministry within their scope of ministry within the team.

It is worth noting that, while the field leadership did not align with the vision of the potential sending church, Global Mission's home director considered such an alignment to be possible. This highlights a genuine issue that can be faced—a situation where the field and mobilisation sides of the same organisation have different perspectives. The reality is that the field has to live with the realities of numerous mobilisation decisions. If either the church or agency is willing to revisit their definition of vision and preferred strategy for ministry, then a partnership could potentially be formed. However, in Ben and Angela's case, as both sides had their own reasons for not compromising on their positions, the partnership did not proceed.

In cases where vision and ministry philosophy do not align, it is perhaps wise to not form a sending partnership to begin with. However, in the case of Christ Community Church and Global Mission, there was a sense of an opportunity lost because possibilities were not fully explored. The lost opportunities lay in the fact that the church valued and desired the agency's missionary care for Ben and Angela, and the agency was keen to receive more workers in this field.

What can help the church and agency work through these differences in vision and ministry philosophy?

Engage the Sending Church

Dialogue between the field leadership and Christ Community Church quickly reached an impasse because the field leaders concluded that, since the local Vietnamese church was already engaged in student ministry, the Singaporean missionaries should do something else. The root of this disconnect is the missiological assumption about what a foreign missionary should do and what the missionary should encourage the local indigenous church to take responsibility for themselves.

While *REMCAP* clearly states that field strategy must be determined by the field leadership, there must also be room to hear a sending church's passion and heartbeat. Field leaders who have had negative experiences with churches that inappropriately dictate their desires for the field may frequently assume that the sending church does not know the reality of field ministry.

Assuming that the church cannot add value to the discussion is not helpful for partnership, as the pastoral responsibility is still a high priority for the church. Also, as church leaders grow in their knowledge of field matters, especially in neighbouring countries where frequent business and travel are conducted, they can be increasingly involved in dialogue and decision-making. While cross-cultural and ministry knowledge may not approach the level of depth of missionaries, a church's desire for ministry and their input should still be respectfully engaged.

Embrace the Whole Agency Family

Christ Community Church initially entered the partnership conversation because it valued the missionary care services of the agency. While this motive was positive, the church leaders asked for the agency's "member care package" thinking that this could be provided while they conducted their own ministry activities and strategies. This approach was not acceptable to the agency. It felt that the church wanted to "pick and choose" from the agency's offering, or worse still, that it was being taken advantage of. Such approaches can create an environment that makes subsequent dialogue more difficult. Missions agencies are reticent to provide piecemeal services, instead desiring missionaries like Ben and Angela to embrace the whole agency family and truly become part of the team.

CMAT members agreed that cherry picking different aspects of a missions agency's offerings is not good practice. It can also be harmful for the missionary. Most agencies have learnt—sometimes through difficult experiences—that mobilisation is an integrated process that can get affected when certain aspects are not included. For example, when a church wants pre-field preparation but not on-field leadership, the missionary is not afforded the full benefit of the partnership.

Some missions agencies make the same mistake of outsourcing their member care entirely to another group. Such practices are less helpful, since the people providing member care are not familiar with neither the culture of the organisation nor its ministry philosophy. The missions agency should serve as an integrated partner of the church, but this does not mean that the agency provides what the church wants in a piecemeal fashion, with the church setting its own vision on the mission field. Instead, the church should send the missionary with its blessing to embrace the missions agency family.

Broaden the Vision

The possibility of collaboration increases when an organisation is willing to broaden its missions vision to encompass a potential partner. Christ Community Church caught a vision of reaching Vietnamese students in a particular locality. The specificity of that vision was due to the church's existing outreach ministry to Vietnamese students, as well as its short-term missions involvement in the same locality in Vietnam.

If the church, including Ben and Angela, broadened its vision to planting Vietnamese faith communities in that city, with student ministry being one of the possible strategies of achieving the vision, this would have changed the tone of conversation between the church and agency. This increased flexibility would have allowed the agency field leaders to explore further possibilities with Christ

Community Church, rather than view it as inflexible in its ministry approach.

A church's vision for ministry in its own community—Singapore for instance—is necessarily specific because it must be tailored to the particular needs, distinctives and context of that particular community. The vision should be specific enough to guide decisions on strategy, but not overly specific as to exclude large segments of the church's diverse membership. In a valiant attempt to be focused on the field, leaders sometimes make the mistake of prescribing an overly specific vision for a church's missions involvement. This mistake often occurs because vision is confused with strategy.

The church may want to do things a certain way and mistakenly states that its vision is primary and therefore should not be changed, when in fact, the manner in which a vision is accomplished can be achieved through various strategies. By correctly identifying strategy as what the church wants done, church leaders would have an improved perspective on whether that strategy is negotiable or not. The cost of a non-negotiable strategy is the exclusion of potential partners and a narrower ministry. This highly specific definition of vision was a factor that prevented Ben and Angela from enjoying the benefits of the missionary care structure of the missions agency.

While Ben and Angela were eventually direct-sent with the specific strategy of student outreach, it is not inconceivable that this strategy may change over time. For example, Christ Community Church may be successful in reaching family members through the students, or graduating students may get married and want to plant their own church. The fact is that strategies necessarily change over time for a variety of reasons, so some flexibility and mutual deference are invaluable in partnership discussions.

Clarify Ministry Philosophy

If the church were to realise that a seemingly immutable vision could be a flexible strategy, could the field leaders of the missions agency have been similarly more flexible in their strategy to include student ministry in their vision? They could not do this because their ministry philosophy was to not engage in a ministry that the local church was already doing and able to accomplish.

In contrast, Christ Community Church held a different ministry philosophy, believing that there was still room for such ministry among the vast numbers of unreached students, even if the local church was already doing it. The purpose of noting this fact is not to argue whether one ministry philosophy is better than the other, but to clearly point out that the core difference that Christ Community Church and Global Mission faced was one of ministry philosophy.

Two organisations that have different approaches to ministry due to differing ministry philosophies would do well to verbalise their philosophy with clarity and their reasons for holding this philosophy. In an inter-organisational relationship, awareness of this difference may sometimes arise only after years of partnership, with great pain and frustration resulting from this divergence. Once leaders see with clarity that the difference is ministry philosophy, two possibilities exist for ministry partnership. First, the ministry philosophies may be different but complementary, with the partnership continuing when the organisations see that their different styles and skills can strengthen the work if they value one another equally. Second, if the ministry philosophies are in conflict with one another and each organisation holds firmly to their respective values, then it is preferable that the partnership not begin in the first place.

CHURCHES ON THE MISSION FIELD

We live in an exciting time when churches are no longer content to take a backseat in missions, leaving all the decisions and involvement to missions agencies. Churches increasingly believe that God has given them a vision for active involvement on the mission field, which goes beyond prayer from afar and having agencies take care of everything for their missionary while they write the cheques.

Such involvement is a positive reflection of the biblical centrality of the church in missions. Many missions agencies welcome this involvement, seeing it as preferable to the sending church lacking involvement with their missionary. However, rules for engagement of the sending church in what has previously been the domain of missions agencies still lack sufficient clarity.

In CMAT, agency leaders recognised that the current environment allows for greater engagement of churches on the mission field. This can be positive, but the local church must be aware of the significant responsibility it bears when it chooses to engage on the field and seek to minister with long-term effectiveness. Some churches have tried to engage heavily on the field or direct-send missionaries without laying a proper missiological foundation. Others have plenty of short-term activity but have not grown the depth or maturity of their involvement. Church leaders should be involved in the strategy of their missionaries if desired, as long as they practise deference to the missions agency's field leaders as the ones who make the call for field decisions. In other words, field leaders in the missions agency make the final decisions regarding ministry of the missionaries sent by the church.

Contributions and Limitations

Many churches send multiple short-term teams in a year, and their leaders have direct, personal relationships with national churches and believers. In Singapore, it is not uncommon for church leaders to have cross-cultural experience and language ability in that field. Coupled with advances in social media, geographical proximity, affordable air travel and globalisation, many churches leaders are familiar with realities on the mission field. In short, their strategic contribution can be real and valuable.

Yet, in spite of all these resources and knowledge—even if commitment and involvement is deep—the sending church must realise that it cannot optimally manage a team or direct its missionaries remotely. In addition, experience in a general region does not always translate into specific contextual understanding in the local culture. Making assumptions about this can lead to ethnocentric mistakes.

Lay leaders in CMAT highlighted that management patterns in secular organisations are often not applicable to cross-cultural missions. In commercial organisations, a CEO can manage a vast network of people via email and video-conferencing, assisted by a large middle-management team, whose performance is measured by key performance indicators and the bottom line. However, in a cross-cultural missionary enterprise, the corresponding middle-management team, and reporting and support structures do not exist. Further, church leaders cannot manage missionaries by setting performance indicators for how many new contacts a missionary makes or how many times the gospel is proclaimed. It should be acknowledged that local success in one's own country does not automatically translate into success in the complexities of cross-cultural work. Allowing field leaders to guide the field strategies is, therefore, necessary.

Direct-Sending Ministry Philosophy

The CMAT leaders did not go as far as to conclude that direct-sending of missionaries by churches is never advisable. There are a number of situations where it may be a reasonable option. For example, in certain mission fields, an agency presence may not exist. Also, if these fields are less complex, it is possible for a direct-sending model to be more workable. Factors that decrease the complexity of a church's missions involvement include language and cultural similarity to those of the sending church, field experience of missionaries and church-leaders, maturity of national church partners, geographic proximity, socio-political stability and ease of acquiring long-term visas for missionaries. Thus, the less complex a mission field, the more likely it is that the sending church is able to successfully direct-send a missionary to that nation.

However, it is valuable to note that the very factors that decrease missions complexity often accompany situations where the target people group has already been reached with the gospel. Correspondingly, churches that prefer to direct-send tend not to work among unreached people groups. Often, sufficiently mature national believers and churches exist in these nations with whom the direct-sending churches seek to partner and minister alongside. Conversely, the more unreached a people group and the more frontier the missions work, the more advisable and valuable it is to have a partnership with a missions agency.

Thus, in areas where the gospel is most needed, partnerships between churches and missions agencies are also the most valuable. Conversely, the choice to use a direct-send approach is more likely to steer a local church away from work among unreached peoples. So, while the effort and intentions of direct-sending churches are commendable, direct-sending of missionaries should not be the sole or preferred method. Instead, it can be one method in the toolbox of sending churches that is appropriate for less complex fields. CMAT, therefore, recommends that churches first seek missions agency partnerships, but keep the option of direct-sending open when missions fields are less complex for the sending church.

The primary downsides of the direct-send strategy are the lack of specialist help, cultural know-how, field structure and established mobilisation processes, which would normally be provided though partnership with missions agencies. Direct-sending has advantages on the home side, with the congregation feeling it is more directly engaged with the work, but the downsides are often felt on the field.

PARTNERSHIP ESSENTIALS

1. The church and missions agency must have aligned vision and ministry philosophy in order to have a successful missionary-sending partnership. Vision is what each organisation seeks to achieve or accomplish on the field. Ministry philosophy is why a church or agency believes it is important to do what it does. It should not be confused with strategy, which is the plans for how an organisation achieves its vision.

2. An important part of the alignment process is understanding that local churches do some things better and mission agencies do other things better. Although working through the diversities can be more time consuming, the benefits of a well-balanced partnership outweigh the extra effort involved. Good dialogue at the start of the partnership building process should

include discussions on what the local church can contribute to the mobilisation effort and what the agency can best support.

3. Strategy alignment is not as essential as vision and ministry philosophy alignment, if church leaders understand that strategies change over time and if they are willing to defer field strategy to field leaders of the missions agency. Good partnerships determine who has the appropriate experience and know-how to make the best decisions at different points of the process. For example, in a crisis situation on the field, a church will be very much involved, but the field leaders are likely to take the leadership in decision-making.

4. An increasing number of churches desire active involvement on the mission field. Their church leaders should engage in discussions on strategy with leaders of the missions agency through whom they are sending their missionaries. Agency leaders should listen carefully and value the input of the church, but the church should still leave the final decisions on field matters to the agency.

5. The church must accept that sending missionaries through a missions agency means embracing the whole agency family. Selecting only certain agency resources or services while retaining the church's own vision and ministry philosophy for the missionary is not advisable.

6. Direct-sending ministry philosophy should not be a preferred missiology for churches. Remote management and decision-making, coupled with weaker missionary care, mean that direct-sending is not optimal for sending missionaries to where

the gospel is the most needed among unreached peoples. In contrast, church-agency partnerships are especially valuable for engaging churches in frontier cross-cultural ministry. Direct-sending should be seen as a method in the toolbox of churches that is suitable for less complex mission fields.

chapter 7

COMMUNICATION & COMMITMENT

Lim Luck Yong & Kelvin Chen

Over a period of two years, Harvest Mission had lost five missionaries sent from various churches. All were serving effectively in teams on the field and enjoyed good support from their field leaders and co-workers. The missionaries were recalled from the field by their churches because the churches no longer wanted to partner with the missions agency.

Each missionary was told that they would no longer be sent in partnership with Harvest Mission. Instead, the churches wanted to direct-send them to the same field where they were currently working. The missionaries were given a choice. If they agreed to this arrangement, their support would be increased, but if they disagreed, their support would cease. In the end, five missionaries complied, leaving the missions agency but returning to the field. A sixth missionary couple decided to remain with Harvest Mission, resulting in their sending church withdrawing financial support.

The churches were frustrated with Harvest Mission because they had been unable to communicate with the home director. Changes in personnel and the lack of a person to fill that role resulted in a silent partnership for over a year. Eventually, they made a unilateral decision to no longer send their missionaries through the agency.

Harvest Mission eventually found a competent director to take up the leadership role, but the churches' decisions to cease partnership had been made and the process was already in motion. Unable to heal the rift in the church-agency relationship, the national director was concerned that this unilateral action of recalling and direct-sending missionaries would damage unity in the body of Christ in both the sending and receiving countries.

ALWAYS NEEDED, OFTEN MISSING

Communication and commitment are components that are always needed, but often missing, for the continuation and maintenance of inter-organisational relationships. A healthy working relationship between the church and missions agency cannot be maintained without both of these elements. Neither party enters the partnership with an intent for it to break down over time, but despite the best intentions and an acknowledgement that partnership is important, communication breakdowns between churches and agencies do happen. At this point, the commitment to sustain the partnership is challenged, sometimes resulting in failed partnerships.

This chapter seeks to unearth the issues that frequently contribute to deteriorating partnerships between the church and missions agency, and to explore good practices for communication and commitment that guard against them. In the context of this chapter, we refer to communication as the exchange of information—verbal, written or otherwise—between the missions leadership of the sending church and that of the missions agency. Commitment refers to the voluntary obligation to one another that the church and agency have entered into in their partnership to send the missionary. Due to the tripartite nature of the sending partnership, communication and commitment are also required between the church and the missionary, as well as between the agency and the missionary. However, the focus of this chapter and this book is the relationship between the church and missions agency.

MISSING PERSONS & CHANGING POLICIES

This case study describes a painful scenario that, unfortunately, is not uncommon. The churches involved underwent a significant change of missions policy during that period. Missionaries were called back home where the church leaders shared their new missions policies. The ministry philosophy of the churches had changed. Previously, the church leaders believed they should work through a missions agency, but now they preferred to send directly from the local church. The fact that the missions agency had not had a national director in place for some time contributed to this change of heart. For a number of years before the withdrawal of the missionaries, there had not been a relationship between the churches and Harvest Mission, because no one in the agency took over the partnership responsibilities of the missing national director.

Church and Agency Perspectives

When the Churches and Missions Agencies Together (CMAT) working group discussed this case study, we first highlighted the distinct perspectives of the church and agency leaders on this topic. Hearing one another helped us better appreciate the frustrations on either side of the church-agency relationship, after which we were able to reach a common understanding on good practice.

Agency leaders in CMAT shared their perception that large churches often desire greater control over their people who are sent through missions agencies. The change in missions policy and the nature of the unilateral decisions of the churches to withdraw their missionaries from the agency appeared to reflect this fact. Agency leaders also highlighted that a sudden withdrawal, as in this case, resulted in great distress for the missionaries despite the fact that the churches allowed them to continue in the same field ministry. Though they returned to the same locations, the missionaries were no longer working with the same teams and friends. Grief and loss frequently occur when missionaries leave their agency family. Though a home director was not designated for an extended period, the field leadership and support of team members of the agency was still in place.

Agency leaders acknowledged Harvest Mission's error of judgment, thinking that the church-agency relationship was satisfactory at the point of separation, but they also expressed hope that churches would consult with the agency and share their unhappiness at an earlier stage. In this manner, mutual decisions could be made in a process of dialogue with one another, rather than a unilateral decision being made by one party to end the partnership.

While agency leaders recognised the frustration that the church leaders must have felt, they also appealed to the churches to consider the consequences of their missions policy and structural changes, especially in light of the ripples created in the field ministry. Agency leaders felt that having a partnership framework, such as the *Relational Model for Church-Agency Partnerships (REMCAP)*, would have greatly helped in such a scenario.

Church leaders in CMAT shared that such a sweeping decision by any church comes only with significant deliberation and pressing reasons. Further, for more than one church to come to the same decision in a similar period reflects the fact that there existed significant problems that were not being dealt with. In this case, with the lack of an agency director to communicate with the church, leaders would have become frustrated that the agency was not providing the necessary support and leadership, which was their responsibility in the partnership. The decision to direct-send their missionaries back to the same field reflects the church leadership's unwavering vision for the ministry, but it also indicates a lack of confidence and trust in the agency.

Underestimating Importance of People and Relationships

Harvest Mission had severely underestimated the negative impact of its lack of a national director. When a missions agency experiences ongoing leadership difficulties, regular communications with partner churches is even more important, and interim measures for this lack of leadership must be put in place. Harvest Mission could have, for example, assigned another capable staff or board member to communicate openly and regularly with partner churches about its challenges and search for a new director.

In *REMCAP*, people and relationships are two of the five key ingredients of church-agency partnerships. On the church side of the relationship, a person may not be assigned to communicate with the agency because church leaders may not know the importance of this ingredient. If no one is identified, for whatever reason, then no personal relationship between the church and agency will exist, resulting in failure of two of the key ingredients of the church-agency partnership. In this perspective, a partnership failure is unsurprising.

CMAT leaders felt that, in this case study, errors had been made on both sides. The agency had not sufficiently communicated with the church for a long period, allowing the people and relationship ingredients to decline. It was also unfortunate that the church made a unilateral decision without consultation with the agency, as this contravenes healthy partnership practice. Commitment does not mean that a partnership can never be ended, but when commitment is rightly questioned, communication should not be neglected. Earlier discussions should be held and prior notice given to the missions agency, even when discontent is warranted.

Communicating More with Missionaries

In addition, church leaders should consult the missionaries affected, rather than make all the decisions on the home side, with the missionaries being passively subject to the change of policy. Certainly, missions agency leaders should also consult missionaries before making significant policy changes that affect them, but this mistake of making missions policy without discussion with missionaries is more frequently made by church leaders.

CMAT noted that though frustrations and hurt were significant for both church and missions agency leaders, emotional pain and ministry disruption were far greater for the missionaries themselves. Therefore, communication and commitment between church and agency leaders directly impacts the missionary care provided to those sent through the church-agency partnership.

Even if a church eventually does decide to withdraw its missionary, early dialogue involving all parties would reduce trauma and mitigate negative impact on the field. When a church changes its missionary-sending policy to become solely direct-sending, CMAT suggests that the church leadership consider permitting current missionaries to continue with the previous missions agency partnership policy, so as to spare them the difficulties associated with the change.

In the CMAT working group, another church leader shared that his church leadership had once considered removing its missionary in a similar situation. The church's frustration was compounded by certain issues on the field, which they felt the agency was not addressing. However, after a series of discussions with the missionary—who was also considering the possibility of leaving the agency's covering—the missions pastor and missionary agreed that, despite the frustrations, the immediate team leader and team members of the agency were providing valuable input and support, so the partnership with the missions agency was retained and subsequently improved.

A Space for Church-Agency Communication

Other members of the working group shared similar stories of churches questioning their earlier commitment to missions agencies. For example, one church had sending partnerships with several agencies; however, its leaders had begun to feel that the agencies and their field leadership were making decisions without sufficient consultation with the sending church, and that the agencies wanted only money and people from the church. Upon discussion, the missions agencies had different perspectives and their leaders tried to explain their actions. Unfortunately, negative impressions had already formed over the years and early communication over these issues had not taken place. Finally, the church leaders decided that they would no longer work with the missions agencies.

All these experiences highlight how communication contributes to a healthy relationship between church and agency leaders. A missing leader results in haphazard communication, if any occurs at all. Frustrations usually do not surface openly until it is too late in the partnership decline. Even in a once healthy relationship, a lack of communication can result in deterioration over time. If a church and agency have regular avenues for communication, with discussion about missions strategy and structure occurring through opportunities such as that provided by a CMAT group, mutual understanding can be promoted. Potential changes in vision, ministry philosophy or strategy can be surfaced for discussion before any final decision is made.

WHY WE COMMUNICATE & COMMIT

The preceding case study helps us better appreciate the gravity of the issue and the factors involved. Although the lack of communication and commitment often leads to a breakdown in partnerships and hampers our efforts in the Great Commission, they are not merely pragmatic issues. Taking a step back, we now consider the deeper motivations for communication and commitment in our partnership relationships.

Reflecting God's Nature

Our involvement in missions entails our being God's ambassadors, representing him to those who do not yet know him. Thus, our character and conduct must reflect this in order to make him known. God shows himself to us continually through the narrative of Scripture, as one who reveals his character, speaks to mankind and commits in covenant to a chosen people. In contrast to inanimate and mute idols, God communicates and covenants with Israel and the Church. Consistent throughout the Old and New Testaments is the revelation that God is patient, slow to anger and abounding in love. He made a costly commitment to save us despite our tendency to wander away from him.

Since our God communicates and covenants with his people, he calls us also to relate to one another in like manner. Within the Christian community, we actively exhort one another to communicate to resolve misunderstandings, forgive wrongs done and honour our commitments to one another, whether in friendship or marriage. Similarly, in inter-organisational relationship between the church and missions agency, CMAT believes that we should likewise reflect God's nature. Our communication with and commitment to one another has practical purpose, but the motivation behind them goes beyond the pragmatic to the reflection of God's character.

Just as our partnership practice should reflect God's relationship with us, it should also reflect the Trinitarian relationship within the Godhead.[13] For this reason, the biblical centrality of the church is held in positive tension with the other values derived from the Trinitarian relationship—equal value of church and agency in missions, glad submission and mutual deference, and joyful fellowship and encouragement.

Truly Valuing One Another

If we value people only for how they can benefit us, the relationship is utilitarian and would fail at the slightest bump. Church-agency partnerships make practical sense for the success of the mission, but relationships that reflect God's nature must go beyond seeing each other as a means to help us achieve our ambitions. When we do not extend ourselves beyond pragmatism, we are committed first to our perceived organisation's success in ministry rather than to the greater kingdom of God and each other as partners. We may even communicate with each other only with the intention of getting the other party to contribute to our goals. Instead of reflecting God's character and Trinitarian nature, our communication and commitment fail to demonstrate true valuing of one other in missions.

Success in Ministry

God is undoubtedly interested in the fruit of ministry success. He desires his Church to reach the lost through a people who reflect his nature. He desires success in church-agency missions through partnerships that bear the marks of glad submission, mutual deference, joyful fellowship and encouragement.[14] However, we must not esteem success of our ministry or organisation as more important than our conduct in ministry partnership.

For example, any leader or organisation will at some point in a partnership make mistakes that may offend the other party or compromise its ministry goals. Our response, whether in judgement or in grace, characterises how we have experienced judgement and grace in our lives. When we do not respond in grace, we foster pride, bitterness and division in the body of Christ. When we esteem our ministry success or that of our organisation above the testimony of a Christ-like response, we contribute to a breakdown of partnerships in missions.

Ultimately, the choice to end a partnership commitment is often a choice of ministry achievements over the relationships established. The more a relationship has deteriorated due to lack of communication, the harder it becomes to maintain that commitment. The more ministry success is valued over commitment, the easier it becomes to forgo a partnership.

ENDING A PARTNERSHIP

If a church-agency partnership does not appear to be furthering the intended ministry or is of insufficient benefit to one party, then how should we assess the possible end of our commitment? First, commitment to a partnership may end when a missionary completes his missionary service and returns home, or the church has no other missionaries or projects with the agency. While transitions can be difficult for the missionary, this "natural ending" of partnership is relatively simple for church and agency leaders to conclude with one another. On the other hand, issues of commitment and communication often arise in situations such as the Harvest Mission case study, where the church is unhappy with aspects of the missions agency, or changes its missions policy. These factors result in the possibility of the church ending the partnership with the missions agency while its missionary is still serving on the field.

Due to the nature of the church-agency relationship—the church being the organisation that sends the resources of people (missionary) and finances to the missions agency—the church is typically the one that questions whether a partnership should continue. This is especially so in the Singapore context, where the sending church frequently provides 50–100% of the missionary's financial support.

Earlier in the chapter, we highlighted the importance and benefits of the church engaging in dialogue with the agency when frustrations arise, instead of making unilateral decisions. *REMCAP* provides a framework on which to assess the current partnership based on agreed upon good practices. Thus, even if a partnership were to eventually end, early dialogue around a common framework would encourage a process that could mitigate damage and trauma.

In making an assessment, however, church leaders must always be cognizant of the distinction between the agency's home leadership and its field leadership. The church may face frustrations with the home front, but if the field is providing strong support to its missionary and if the missionary wishes to stay with the agency, then these points must factor strongly into the assessment. Ultimately, while the decision to end a partnership often rests primarily with the church leadership, the missionary is the person who ultimately pays the highest price.

PARTNERSHIP ESSENTIALS

1. Continuous communication to maintain the commitment between church and missions agency is always needed, but often missing, in church-agency partnerships.

2. In a church-agency partnership, people and relationships are the two key ingredients that will maintain healthy levels of communication and commitment. The wrong person or the lack of a person in the leadership role will inevitably result in deterioration of the church-agency relationship.

3. Our communication and commitment to one another has essential practical benefits, but our motivations must go deeper than pragmatism. God communicates with and commits to his chosen people. Therefore, we reflect God's nature when we communicate with and commit to one other.

4. Success of our ministry or organisation should not be deemed more important than our conduct in ministry partnership. Commitment to ministry success is misplaced, as is communication with others in order to manipulate them to help us succeed. Reflecting God's nature means that we value partnership relationships above immediate ministry success.

5. The CMAT group format and process provides a space for regular communication between the church and agency. The guiding framework allows frustrations to be surfaced and resolved by raising issues in case studies for group discussion. This allows partnership understanding and commitment to grow, which is invaluable when greater crises arise.

6. When assessing the possibility of ending a partnership, churches should involve the missionary in the deliberations and engage the missions agency earlier rather than later. As missionaries encounter the greatest change and stress in such a scenario, their input should be factored into the assessment.

chapter 8

MISSIONARY CANDIDATURE & PREPARATION

Jeffrey Lum, Paul Tan & Thomas Lim

Vivian, who had been serving with her church on staff, was interested in ministry in Cambodia. She received permission from the church missions committee to apply to a missions agency. The church-agency partnership was a new relationship, and meetings were arranged for the leaders to discuss Vivian's candidature. The church leaders appeared hesitant about sending Vivian as a missionary. Citing a lack of accountability on her part, they wanted more time to assess her. Meanwhile, the missions agency leaders had identified a mentor to journey with Vivian. They also recommended that she strengthen relationships with her church, especially the leaders, and continue to share about why she felt called to the mission field.

While the church took time to assess Vivian, meetings between the church and agency leaders continued. Vivian continued her mentorship in the missions agency and made trips to Cambodia to confirm her burden for the ministry. The agency's field leader visited Singapore, spoke at Vivian's church and met the leaders. However, the church decided to delay sending Vivian. The delay was first one year and then increased to three years; this was compounded by leadership changes in the church. With no further development on her sending, Vivian felt frustrated with the situation. Eventually, she withdrew her application from the agency.

READY, GET SET, BUT NO GO!

Every so often, we rejoice that someone has heard God's call and dedicates his or her life to cross-cultural missions. However, in this case study, an issue arose in the process of candidature within the church. This issue had to be dealt with while the candidature with the agency continued at a faster pace than the church's assessment process. When the agency was almost ready to send, concerns among church leaders resulted in shifting delay that eventually became three years. Furthermore, Vivian's assessment became lost amidst changes in church leadership. This resulted in great frustration for Vivian, who eventually withdrew her application as everything ground to a halt.

The church and missions agency should work in tandem to approve and send any candidate, but something went amiss in the early stage of partnership formation as various leaders considered Vivian's candidature. This chapter will explore the partnership issues that surround candidature, where potential missionaries are prepared, assessed and approved by leaders in two partnering organisations.

The "missionary call" is a deeply personal conviction of God's purpose for the life work of a person in missions. People who sense such a call of God to missions and apply to be missionaries, usually in a cross-cultural setting, are called "missionary candidates". The local church at which they are members is made aware of this call and provides support toward their application to become missionaries. When the candidates apply to be missionaries with a missions agency, they need to follow a number of agency procedures and meet certain requirements before they are accepted as missionaries. Similarly, a church typically has its own processes, though often less detailed or structured than those of the agency, as church leaders have often observed the candidate in lay ministry for a number of years. This whole application and approval process is known as candidature.

COMMUNICATING & ADDRESSING CONCERNS

Since missions candidature is a long journey with potential pitfalls along the way, active communication between church and agency leaders regarding the progress of the candidature is extremely helpful. Although Vivian's church leaders met with those from the agency, it appears that deeper concerns were not expressed. In what ways was Vivian's church ready, or not ready, to journey with her in sending her as a missionary? What aspects of the relationship among the church, missions agency and missionary candidate contributed to this unfortunate situation? What could the missions agency or church have done differently to better handle such a situation?

On the positive side, the church was ready to consider sending Vivian and to talk with a missions agency about what this would involve. However, the leadership's communication with Vivian appeared to be lacking at multiple levels. If church leaders have concerns about a potential missionary's suitability, they must talk through these concerns with their own member before engaging the missions agency. This does not mean to say that a church must have all the boxes checked before approaching an agency. Rather, major concerns should be settled first so that when a candidate applies to the missions agency, the church can support the member while requesting for the agency's help in working through the candidate's weaknesses. In this manner, candidature is done in partnership, rather than with the church struggling to approve Vivian on their end while church-agency talks are simultaneously proceeding.

While Singaporeans are more direct than many other Asians, we are still Asian in our expression of concerns or problems. Thus, if a church says, "Hold on and take time", it usually means there are serious concerns that will not automatically be dealt with by the mere passage of time. Furthermore, we often find it difficult to bring the concerns directly to the missionary candidate. However, in such cases, it is the responsibility of the church leadership to do so. Cultural communication preferences are not a reasonable excuse to withhold telling missionary candidates one's concerns about them before their application to a missions agency. By giving permission for Vivian to apply to the agency, the church leadership was sending confusing signals, resulting in bad communication.

A third area of failed communication happened throughout the three-year period of evaluation. Although such a waiting period is common for missionary candidates, regular official communication must be a part of this process. As Vivian had not received regular updates about this issue of accountability, delays were understandably frustrating and confusing for her. This difficulty was compounded by leadership changes in the church, highlighting the need for clear policies so that a missionary candidate can continue to be processed even though there may be a change in senior pastor, missions pastor or missions chairman.

While there is room for improvement in communication on the part of the church leadership, their actual decision was prudent and wise. With their long-term experience with Vivian, both as a church member and staff, they should rightfully address those concerns before sending her to the field. Churches often have a longer and deeper relationship with candidates than the agency. Thus, it is wise of the church leadership to say "not yet" and express willingness to journey with the missionary candidate. However, clarity must be evident in the process and final decision. The church leadership must be able to give a definitive answer in the end; unfortunately, in this case, the communication petered out.

In this case study, the missions agency was very proactive, and some of that initiative was shown to be mutually demonstrated by the church—continued meetings, approval given to Vivian to make field visits through the missions agency and visits from the field leader to Vivian's church. If there was any mistake made, it was perhaps that the missions agency misjudged the severity of the church's concerns and moved too quickly. Like in any relationship, partnership development must be in tandem and the foundational concerns of one party must be addressed. Though the church identified accountability as a foundational issue, the agency had gone ahead to arrange field visits, obtain approval of the area leader to receive Vivian and assign a mentor to Vivian. The foundational issue—why the church perceived that Vivian had an issue with accountability and how this could be resolved—was not addressed.

As this case involved a new relationship between the church and agency, we have especially highlighted the importance of the church and missions agency both moving at a similar pace of readiness when preparing to send a new missionary to the field. One contributing factor for the church leaders' hesitancy to send Vivian could be the realisation of the accountability lines within the church-agency partnership that was potentially forming. When partnering with an agency, the issue of Vivian's accountability becomes more apparent. While the church leadership could overlook some concerns about

Vivian when she was on staff, they would need to have much more confidence in her in order to send her to the field through an agency, where there is greater freedom and less oversight by the church.

In summary, the church could have journeyed better with Vivian. A mentor from the church could have been assigned to communicate church concerns and the progress of candidature. Foundational concerns should be openly discussed and addressed; otherwise, the missionary would feel increasingly frustrated in trying to move ahead while being held back by the foundational concern. When the candidature process is conducted in partnership, the church and agency should progress at similar levels of commitment and approval of the missionary. If the church has foundational concerns, then the agency must share those foundational concerns and address them first.

EVALUATING & PREPARING CANDIDATES

The four Cs of calling, character, competence and communication can provide a helpful framework when evaluating and preparing missionary candidates. In each of these areas, both the church and agency have particular and unique contributions toward a candidate.

Both the church and agency should pay close attention to God's call on potential missionaries. Their character must also be given due consideration. As people living and witnessing for Christ on the mission field, who they are speaks louder than the message that they seek to bring to the people.

If a missionary candidate fails in competency on home ground, how can the person be expected to thrive on the mission field? Finally, as highlighted in the case study, communication—an important element in the candidature process and the preparation phase of the missionary candidate—can either move the process forward or hinder it.

Calling

A clear sense of calling is important, as it enables the church to confirm and affirm that calling. At times, the calling may not be very direct or evident, but God can be seen clearly guiding the candidate into full-time ministry through life events or circumstances. The candidate may gain greater clarity concerning God's direction by carefully processing the circumstances that led to the possibility of missions service. This has to be confirmed and affirmed by the missions committee or board and the agency that the candidate seeks to join.

From the agency perspective, the call may be further affirmed through the candidature process. For instance, in the process of discerning with the candidate a possible placement on the field (whether in a specific location or working with a particular team), all parties may come to see God's direction for the potential missionary. Another indication of the calling is God's provision in enabling a candidate to raise full financial support and to enlist committed prayer partners. Both the church and agency share in this responsibility to ascertain and affirm that call.

Character

The church should know the candidate—perhaps not known personally by the senior leadership, but at least by members with whom he or she has been serving. The candidate should at least have been with the church for two to three years, thus allowing the church to attest to the candidate's personality, contribution and effectiveness in ministry.

There might also be a time of interning in the church to hone and sharpen the candidate's ministry skills through serving in different areas of ministry. This would help the candidate to build relationships with more church members and, in return, the church members to become acquainted with the potential missionary. All these will help the leaders to assess the candidate's suitability and affirm his or her call to cross-cultural ministry. If there are concerns, the church would have to manage accordingly. In time to come, when the candidate is raising support, more church members will be willing to pray and give financially.

To the agency, each candidate who submits an application typically starts off as an unknown person with an unknown character. The challenge for the agency is to get to know the person more deeply, in terms of skills (people/relational skills, gifts, talents), training received (secular, professional, specialised, bible school), character and experiences (in ministry, spiritual gifting and cross-cultural context). Such information could be gleaned through application papers, interviews and interactions with the candidate, as well as through feedback from references. With time spent relating to and observing the candidate, the agency can grow to better understand the candidate and assess her effectively.

Since the church often knows the candidate better than the agency, it is able to provide valuable input for the candidature process. In a separate case discussed by the Churches and Missions Agencies Together (CMAT) leaders, when leaders of one church felt that a particular candidate was not ready to be sent, they shared their concerns with the missions agency. Since the candidate was already in an application process with the agency, the church requested that the candidature process be kept on hold while they continued to journey with and mentor their member. After a few years, the church gave the candidate approval to continue candidature, and the missionary was eventually accepted and sent to the mission field.

With regard to missionary assessment, the missions agency typically has a more thorough protocol. This may include personality tests, psychological assessments and references from the candidate's leaders, friends and pastor. When the agency finds areas that the candidate needs to address before going to the field, the church should work with the agency to deal with these issues.

If this process necessitates a delay and more time is needed, neither the church nor agency should seek to rush the process with the other organisation. The missions agency should similarly not deal hastily with the church's concerns, or vice versa, because issues that are not properly dealt with will eventually surface when stress arises during cross-cultural ministry. Even then, thoroughly dealing with issues to the satisfaction of all parties is not a guarantee that candidates will navigate through future trials successfully. However, early preparation reduces the chance of a crisis and premature return from the field.

Competency

Part of evaluating the candidate involves determining the person's physical and emotional state of health. Both the church and agency should be concerned with this aspect of a candidate's readiness, and sharing this information helps foster trust between the church and missions agency. Ministry on the mission field is spiritual in nature and involves spiritual warfare in one form or another. To be fully equipped, the candidate has to be spiritually prepared in body, mind and soul. Understanding the candidate's state of health and emotional-psychological well-being would help everyone to ascertain whether the potential missionary is prepared to face the rigours of the mission field. This shared knowledge of the candidate's competency will enable the church and agency to prepare the potential missionary to thrive and remain for as long as possible on the mission field.

In the broadest sense, the preparation of candidates begins even before they speak with their church leaders or make an enquiry with the agency. God often uses the candidates' past experiences as part of their preparation to serve on the mission field. This informal preparation should be taken into account during the candidature process, and additional formal means of preparation is recommended. Both the church and agency must agree on the plan for this formal preparation, and jointly supervise the candidate.

As the potential missionary progresses through the candidature process and nears the point of becoming a full member of the agency sent to the field, this joint supervision is increasingly undertaken by the missions agency. This aligns with the *Relational Model of Church-Agency Partnership (REMCAP)* analogy of "church family at home" and "agency family at work". A person is released from their "home to the "workplace" where their field ministry is under the supervision of the missions agency.

• • •

In ensuring the candidate's competency to arrive on the field as well prepared as possible, the following areas require attention:

Acquiring skills/knowledge. Informally, a period of internship in a church setting or ministry involvement to gain experience—both of which would be best supervised by the church—will help the candidate. Formally, this may involve seminary studies, pre-field cross-cultural training, or professional specialised training. For example, Asia Cross-Cultural Training Institute (ACTI) and School of Frontier Missions (SoFM) are popular pre-field training programmes in Singapore, whereas Teaching English to Speakers of Other Languages (TESOL) is an internationally recognised certification that is often helpful in the mission field.

Growing in personal development. Developing oneself requires discipline and intentionality. Candidates need to possess these two traits when serving on the mission field. Personal growth could be attained through mentoring sessions, reading and reflecting on books or articles, and attending seminars or workshops. Spiritual formation is an ongoing process in any disciple and this is assumed to be also true for the missionary candidate.

Being aware of the mission field context. The candidate can arrange with the church or the agency for an exploratory trip to the field. Information on the field context and current ministry situation is available to help engage prayer partners and supporters. Today, we have no lack of resources that a candidate can draw from.

Taking practical steps. The agency is responsible to prepare the candidate at various stages—from candidature to arrival on the field. The first of many orientations would be a candidate course, to help candidates better understand the agency and its ministry/workings, as well as how to serve in accordance with its practices, ministry philosophy and values. Other practical matters that require a missionary's attention are:

1. Writing regular prayer letters to ensure the supporting community knows what the candidate is going through, from

candidature to service on the field. As a candidate seeking to raise prayer partners and financial support, the prayer letter is an important medium of communication with the sending and supporting community.

2. Making decisions relating to children's education and a host of other child-related issues for those going to the field with their families.

3. Leaving the care of people, possessions and properties in a responsible way. This may include the appointment of a guardian, a support network to care for aged parents, or giving someone power of attorney.

4. Bringing about closures such as farewells, dealing with necessary issues, and ensuring that sufficient time has been given to the grieving of losses.

Communication

When a candidate feels that God is moving him or her to serve as a missionary, the church leaders should be informed sooner, rather than later. This gives church leaders more time to assess and walk with the candidate.

At times, a potential candidate may share with church leaders an interest in the mission field, even though she is clearly too young or immature. Instead of dismissively telling the young person to take a few years to think about it, church leaders would be wise to journey with the person and encourage informal means of preparation through ministry service and life experience. The church may also want to engage a missions agency that can provide experienced missionaries to mentor the candidate.

Even when a candidate is ready to be mentored, churches often do not have the people with the needed experience to mentor potential missionaries. Though church leaders have a duty to help a member clarify God's call on her life, the same leaders may not be able to connect with the cross-cultural interests of the candidate. Existing missionaries of the church are likely on the mission field and not able to mentor the candidate. Early partnership with a missions agency can be highly valuable to a church at this point, for most agencies are more than willing to mentor such a person even though she may not be ready to apply to the agency, and there is no guarantee that she would be sent out through that agency.

When the church and agency take up their respective roles to clarify a candidate's call, communication between the church and agency is established. Although the candidate may not eventually go with that agency, from a kingdom perspective, there is still much to rejoice, because the process itself will build and strengthen partnership among the church, agency and candidate.

Vivian's case highlights the need to have in place a process for handling a concern in the candidate's life or ministry. When either the church or agency identifies a concern, leaders from both organisations should agree on the nature of this concern and the process for addressing it in consultation with the missionary candidate. This process must include clear articulation of the concern to the candidate, expectations during the candidature, and checkpoints in this journey where feedback is given. Leaders must emphasise that the goal of this process is to develop the candidate and not to hold her back from the field.

Bob was a missionary candidate who wanted to serve in a country known for being a difficult field due to high levels of spiritual and psycho-emotional challenges. Although Bob was applying to initially serve for only a two-year commitment, the agency felt that in this specific context, Bob should be spiritually prepared through some formal training. Thus, in agreement with the church, Bob first completed an internship as a church staff to allow leaders to observe him, followed by one year of bible school training. Though Bob's deployment to the field was set back by two years, the process was agreed upon by all parties and the time was an essential part of his preparation.

PARTNERSHIP ESSENTIALS

1. Biblical centrality of the church is reflected in the practice that the church must affirm the calling, character and competency of the candidate. The church sends the missionary, so the church should affirm and approve him.

2. Candidature is best processed by the church and agency together, rather than the church having an entirely separate process before handing a candidate to the agency. The church often has longer and deeper relationships with the candidate, but it equally values the missions agency's structured candidature protocol, experience in assessing the missionary call, specialist input and ability to equip for competency.

3. The church should ideally have a process for approving and selecting members to be missionary candidates. This process can include engaging missions agencies at an early stage to give increased missions exposure to candidates and provide mentors for them. The agency's candidature process should be made clear to the candidate and the church from the start.

4. When church leaders have reservations about a candidate, this process should include sharing concerns openly with the agency. The agency should not be expected to uncover suitability problems of the candidate on its own. Likewise, the agency should seek clarification from the church before beginning the candidature process, carefully listening to any concerns expressed.

5. Leaders of both the church and missions agency should come to an agreement regarding any concern about the candidate that either organisation raises. The process to address this concern must be discussed and agreed upon by the leaders together with the missionary candidate. Communication of this concern should focus on encouraging development of the candidate even if this means a delay in deployment to the field.

6. Cooperation between the church and agency is evidenced in personal communication between the leaders throughout the selection, assessment and preparation of the missionary candidate through both informal and formal means of equipping.

7. Candidates should, therefore, not be "caught in the middle", feeling responsible to balance both church and agency policies. Church and missions agency leaders are responsible for ensuring that their organisations are in alignment at each stage of candidature, not the missionary candidates themselves.

8. New church-agency partnership should be nurtured through face-to-face meetings between the respective leaders as early in the relationship as possible. Alignment of vision and ministry

philosophy of the church and agency must be established first before the potential missionary begins candidature.

9. The value of joyful fellowship and encouragement is evidenced in personal relationships between church and agency leaders, and with the candidate. Trust in the good intentions of leaders helps greatly when challenges come along the way, and concerns and disappointments must be dealt with.

chapter 9

FINANCES

Ivan Liew & Leonard Leow

Michael and Jennifer had faithfully served in Japan for more than 15 years. When they first left Singapore, the newly married couple were thankful for the financial support they received, which met their basic needs. Now, they have teenage children and are thinking further into the future. They have an apartment in Singapore but insufficient savings for retirement or medical emergencies. Their sending church and missions agency are also considering policies for additional financial support that would meet at least some of their medical, housing and personal needs as they age.

Both church and agency leaders desired equitable and mutually agreeable good practice, but challenges needed to be addressed. The agency had its own financial policy it wanted to implement, but their missionaries are sent by various churches that view the retirement provision issue differently. The agency decided to communicate to all the churches that they would begin increasing the support budgets of missionaries because of this retirement savings component.

Michael and Jennifer's church leaders agreed to the rationale of some increase, but they felt that the amount recommended by the missions agency was too high. The church felt a missionary's retirement support should be benchmarked against what other church staff were receiving and also take into account the substantial rental income that the couple was receiving from their home in Singapore.

These different views needed to be resolved in time for Michael and Jennifer's budget the following year, and in a way that was mutually acceptable to both the church and agency. Further, as the leaders were aware that the policy changes and process could be stressful for Michael and Jennifer, they wanted to decide and implement this in a manner that would be viewed as positive missionary care rather than negative stressors.

MONEY IS AN IMPORTANT TABOO

A successful partnership between the church and missions agency cannot occur without good practices and a common understanding with regard to the handling of finances. Next to human resource, money is the next most valuable resource exchanged between the church and missions agency. *The Relational Model of Church-Agency Partnerships (REMCAP)* describes finances as one of the key elements in a church and agency partnership, because church and missions agency leaders repeatedly point to finance matters when describing their partnership relationships.

Thus, money is both unavoidably important and yet a taboo subject in a church-agency relationship. We raise the issue hesitantly and only when we must. Missionaries and agency leaders usually talk about it apologetically when they need to ask the church for more money. Church leaders often have questions or concerns that they would never raise directly with the agency, because they fear it will become divisive. Simmering tensions rise, which either erupt when a crisis occurs or become the unhealthy norm in an uneasy partnership that never reaches its full potential.

In Singapore, every employee has some of their salary set

aside in "forced savings" called the Central Provident Fund (CPF). The government also adds to each person's CPF account, so every Singaporean has something they can withdraw at retirement. Many missionaries, especially those sent to the field decades ago, never had provisions for retirement and therefore very little CPF savings during all the years they were on the field. As a result, some could not afford to return to Singapore or chose to retire on the mission field. Others, like Michael and Jennifer, still have many more years of missionary service, and their church and agency are trying to change financial policies while they are on the field.

This chapter will deal with the concerns of finances that arise when a long-term missionary is sent through a partnership between a church and missions agency. We will not consider finances for short-term missions or financial partnerships for ministry projects. With the focus on long-term missionary sending, Michael and Jennifer's case study of retirement savings will be analysed together with other examples. While this topic is necessarily broad, the principles and good practices described will be helpful to church and agency leaders as they approach this potentially thorny issue.

For these reasons, Michael and Jennifer's missions agency leaders approached the increase of their retirement support with prayerful trepidation. They knew that some of their partner church relationships had unspoken tensions related to finances, and this new policy may increase underlying tensions. Leaders in Churches and Missions Agencies Together (CMAT) agreed on certain good practice guidelines for retirement savings, and outlined ways to resolve differences when organisations disagree or have differing policies.

RETIREMENT & HOME OWNERSHIP

Some missionaries return to their home country after 30 years on the field with health issues, no home to their name, no savings for increasing medical costs and nothing set aside for years of retirement. CMAT agreed that churches and missions agencies should look to providing a retirement component for missionaries and consider home ownership, particularly for Singaporean missionaries. Though it may not be a large amount in absolute terms, allocating retirement and home ownership components in support raising legitimises the need and is extremely helpful for the missionary.

Retirement Support Component

Savings toward retirement is best considered as part of a missionary's regular support budget and built into it when a missionary is first sent. This provision is not necessary for short-term workers with one- to two-year commitments, but long-term missionaries need this component when they first go to the field, otherwise they will have no retirement savings after decades of missionary service.

In Singapore, it is common practice to base the retirement component on the CPF, assuming a median salary in Singapore, or a comparable salary of a church staff based in Singapore. Some churches set up missionary retirement savings accounts to which these amounts are deposited, or deposit directly into the missionary's CPF account. Other churches purchase insurance policies that not only cover medical and evacuation emergencies, but also provide an endowment so the missionaries would eventually receive cash for their retirement. Whatever the method chosen, the principle agreed upon is that retirement funds based on the home country must be factored into a long-term missionary's budget, even if the resulting amount is surprisingly higher compared to the much lower living expenses on the mission field.

Home Country Cost of Living

The amount of the retirement component must be based on the cost of living of the home country to which the missionary returns. The rationale is that the missionary will return to the home country, so budgeting must take into account the often more expensive home country and not only the cost of living on the field. Even if a missionary does not plan to retire at home, visa issues, changing socio-political realities, and medical emergencies sometimes necessitate the return to home.

For Singaporean missionaries, their CPF component can increase their budgets by as much as 30%. The higher the cost of living of the home nation as compared to the field nation, the greater percentage increase of these home or retirement components. Consequently, the larger this percentage, the greater the "sticker shock" and the more difficult it is for a church to accept why a missionary should raise this budget when they are ministering in a field with a low cost of living.

Home Ownership and Savings

Long-term Singaporean missionaries are counselled and highly encouraged to purchase a Housing Development Board (HDB) apartment before departing for the mission field. Many missionaries, especially married couples, are able to put a down-payment on a simple HDB flat, and the rental income while they are serving on the field is more than sufficient to cover the mortgage. The result is additional savings from the rental income, and a roof over their heads when missionaries eventually return home. In retirement, the large value stored in their homes helps greatly with financial security, and provides additional income through renting out a room or, in the case of government housing in Singapore, selling back some of the remaining lease to the government for additional income even while one continues to live in the home.

Some missionaries, especially singles, may not be able to afford an HDB flat when they leave for the mission field. In such cases, it is important that sufficient funds be raised for the missionary so that they can purchase a home when the time comes. For example, a 25-year-old single missionary first sent to Cambodia may not own an apartment in Singapore, but when she gets married at 30 years of age, her savings should allow her to make a down-payment on an HDB flat with her future husband. If she turns 35 and becomes eligible to purchase a Singapore government apartment as a single, she should have enough savings to make this down-payment. Therefore, she must be counselled at age 25 to raise sufficient support, and be backed by her church and missions agency to do so.

FINANCES AS MISSIONARY CARE

When a church and missions agency guide and provide for their missionary in these financial matters, the missionary receives a highly positive form of missionary care. The role of the sending church is particularly crucial in this matter. If a church says, "Go in peace, be warm and filled" but does little for its missionary's financial needs, then what good is that? (James 2:16) On the other hand, effective missionary care in the area of finances occurs when a church has in place missions policies that provide for their workers, and leadership that acts as their advocates.

High Percentage of Support

Many churches in Singapore support their missionary with significant percentages of their support budgets. It is not uncommon for the sending church to provide 50–100% of their missionary's agency-approved budget. One of the churches in CMAT shared its model of support-raising, which it found works particularly well. Its missionaries are sent through multiple agencies. Fifty percent of their budget is provided from the missions budget of the church, while the remaining 50% is raised from the congregation. The missions pastor leads the annual call to pledge to missionaries, so the missionaries do not have to canvas for support. With the church leadership giving the call for missions giving, 100% of missionary support is raised from within the church, with many people being repeat supporters over many years.

Further, the congregation gives their money to a designated account for the missionaries in the local church, resulting in two benefits. First, the church sends the entire sum to the missions agency, thus strengthening the church-agency relationship and reflecting the central role of the local church in the missionary-sending endeavour. Second, surplus funds can be reserved for urgent needs or important future items, such as study expenses, so that annual budgets are not sharply increased. This arrangement has proven highly effective in providing for missionaries, engaging the congregation and showing comprehensive financial missionary care.

Continuing Support at Home

Specific areas where financial policies are particularly important in missionary care are home-assignments, re-entry transitions, sabbaticals and courses for study. CMAT highlights to churches that financial support should not stop when missionaries are away from their field in their home country. Some churches stop their support immediately when a missionary returns from the field, unknowingly causing great difficulty for the missionary.

At certain life stages, such as when teenage children enter university or 18-year-old Singapore males begin their military National Service, an extended home assignment of one to two years may be necessary. A sending church should have a policy to continue support and work with the missions agency on the missionary's ministry assignment, which could be with the church or with the agency, or a combination of both. When a missionary leaves the field, especially if this departure is unexpected and stressful due to illness or visa issues, churches within CMAT provide for continued financial support for 3–12 months, which allows time for the missionary to process re-entry issues and perhaps transition to a new ministry field.

Parental Support

An additional missionary care issue, which is important for those from Asian backgrounds, is providing financial support to parents at home, many of whom are non-Christians. Though this may seem unnecessary to western cultures, providing regular financial giving to parents is essential in many Asian cultures. Even if some parents are financially independent, giving a small amount is seen as filial piety in action. Especially since the missionaries are not at home to visit their ageing parents, this expression of love and care is highly valuable and should therefore be factored into a missionary's budget. Church leaders should support this, especially since church members are the ones in the best position to visit the same parents at key times such as when the elderly fall ill or at Lunar New Year celebrations.

Additional Needs

In the event that a missionary is blessed to receive more than sufficient funds, a church or missions agency can set this aside for future needs such as sabbaticals and study programmes. Within CMAT, one of the church-agency partnerships had successfully seen three experienced missionaries complete postgraduate study programmes while on the field or during home assignments. This would not have been possible without both church and agency support, including policies on both sides that allowed the raising of funds for study needs.

FLEXIBLE SUPPORT LEVELS

Thus far, this chapter has cited all positive examples, but the reality is that not all missionaries and not all churches are able to raise complete financial support, even if the pastor advocates for the missionary and the congregation is willing to give. CMAT recommends that agencies adopt the practice of having flexible levels of support for their missionaries and that churches understand how these different levels impact their missionaries. If a missions agency has insufficient support-raising guidelines, adopting an extreme "by faith" policy, then they are neither guiding their missionaries nor giving them the needed coverage or backing to raise such funds from their churches and individual supporters.

One particular missions agency in CMAT has three different levels of support for all its workers heading to the field – Minimal, Base and Maximum. All new workers must raise their funds up to the Minimal level before they can be sent out. This level represents the bare minimum for life and ministry on the field. The Base level is more realistic and includes long-term needs such as health insurance and savings toward retirement. Singapore missionaries are encouraged to consider the Singapore government's guidelines for a "minimum sum" of CPF savings for their retirement. Most will not budget or raise the full CPF amount as compared to employees in Singapore, but setting aside a fixed amount monthly (e.g. S$500–800 per person) is highly encouraged. Another agency sets a recommended minimum of S$500 per individual for such savings, with flexibility to go higher if the supporting church permits this. These amounts are reviewed periodically to ensure they are realistic in light of future needs.

DIFFERENCES & DISAGREEMENTS

Even when both the church and missions agency agree to the good practice guidelines above, there exists plenty of room for disagreement in the area of finances, especially on the amount to be raised and the rationale behind this budgeted amount. Finances is an indisputably key element in partnership, yet leaders approach this topic hesitantly because past experiences reveal that churches and agencies may view these differently. To resolve these differences, there must first be a recognition of valuing one another equally in the missions endeavour. CMAT principles guide leaders to see that both churches and agencies have needed perspectives that must be brought to the table.

In Michael and Jennifer's case, the missions agency first raised the issue of increasing the CPF and retirement savings component with the church. The partnership had pre-existing good relationships and mutual trust, so raising this topic was not difficult. The agency leaders had a suggested figure, which they said they wanted to slowly raise over the next five years.

Michael and Jennifer's support was coming entirely from their home church, a common scenario in Singapore. The church agreed to increase the support figure, but it wanted a different means of calculation that also increased the support of its other missionaries sent through different agencies. It also wanted to take into account factors such as the salary of church staff and home rental income. The church's logic was that missionaries were receiving substantial rental income while a home was being provided for them on the field, a benefit which church staff did not receive.

The agency's policy was to not take so many elements into account, but their policy did stipulate that the primary sending church would have the final decision. Thus, they deferred to the church, knowing that the church had a good policy in place, even though this policy was different from that of the agency. Michael and Jennifer's budget was calculated slightly differently from some other missionaries sent from the same agency.

Biblical centrality of the church does not mean that the church always has the final say in financial matters. While the Singapore context features many missionaries supported by one church, there are many missionaries whose support comes from many churches and individuals, with no single church having a strong say in the finances. In such cases, the missions agency has the primary responsibility to consider financial issues such as retirement savings, and the missionary has a greater responsibility to raise this sum.

One of the best ways to learn and improve policies is through proven good practices of others. Within CMAT, sharing stories and good practices helped churches and agencies to both learn new ideas from one another and affirm existing good policy. For example, while discussing Michael and Jennifer's case, two churches shared that they had missionaries serving for more than 20 years on the field. When they increased the retirement component, they realised that their long-serving missionaries had been "short-changed" for the past 20 years. Being financially strong, the churches decided on a one-time payment to these missionaries. Another church did the same when they realised that their retired missionary's savings account was very low because they had not been raising funds for it for the past 25 years. As can be imagined, the thought and effort behind such a gift was immensely appreciated by the missionaries as a valuable form of missionary care.

CHALLENGES & FINANCIAL REALITIES

The CMAT leaders who recommended these good practices were fully aware of the challenges faced by the field workers, as many had been missionaries themselves. Some felt the heavy burden of having to raise funds for their retirement. When missionaries have a financial shortfall for their regular monthly support, the furthest thing on their minds is setting aside some money for their retirement fund. Other missionaries struggle to raise the minimal amount to be sent to the field, so having to look into raising money for their retirement places more pressure on them.

Some churches that desire to support their missionaries more fully are themselves struggling financially and thus cannot sufficiently support them to the recommended amount. In such a scenario, the church leaders may allow the missionaries to raise the amount that they need through personal contacts outside the supporting church. To some extent, missionaries also need to exercise a certain level of faith, trust and dependence on the Lord for their needed finances. Even sending countries like Singapore, which are financially strong now, will have to deal with the future realities of an ageing population and lower birth rates, which will impact missions support.

Even after missionaries have raised sufficient support to be deployed on the field, economic uncertainties and national crises can have a huge impact on them. Tumbling exchange rates result in a decrease of support, even when the home country is still giving the same amount in their home currency. In a global financial crisis, missionaries' finances are drastically reduced. These scenarios have forced many missionaries to return to their home countries prematurely.

Such financial difficulties can be a deterrent for potential new missionaries who must step out in faith, but when church and agency leaders work together to care for existing missionaries, where robust policies are in place and when God provides for faith-filled missionaries, the next generation is inspired, assured and strengthened to press on. Church leaders must be cognizant of the high financial cost of supporting long-term missionaries and prepare their members for the commitment needed to be a sending and supporting church.

ROLES & RESPONSIBILITIES

We can increase clarity regarding the finances of sending partnerships by highlighting the respective roles of the missions agency as responsible advocates, the church as caring financial providers, and the missionary and the missionary as a responsible partner in personal finances.

The Missions Agency as Advocates

Though different agencies have diverse policies regarding financial support, the agency (and not the church) must be the organisation that advocates for financial needs such as retirement provision. Since retirement savings should be considered as part of regular support, the agency must communicate this to both the missionary and sending church during candidate discussions. A retirement and home ownership plan should be in place before the missionary is sent to the field.

For new missionaries, this may be the last thing on their mind when they are struggling to raise funds for their basic support, but the agency should educate new workers on a viable plan for the future. Even if it means setting aside just a small amount, such as few hundred dollars a month, this would grow to a substantial sum over the years and provide a good basis for future fundraising.

The agency must also be an advocate for the missionary to the sending church. Churches may not think of this retirement component when sending a missionary, or may have no idea how to calculate an appropriate amount when sending their first members as missionaries. The agency has the indispensable responsibility to advocate for a reasonable amount. This principle applies to other areas of finances, not just retirement savings. A missionary would find it difficult to ask for more funds or raise more money for what may be seen as personal or non-urgent needs, but if ministry on the field reveals a genuine need for finances, or long-term realities at home that more money be raised, then the missions agency must advocate for the missionary.

When the agency develops policy, it must consider how this will be communicated and received. On the one hand, extremes of "living by faith" without appropriate guidelines does not help a new sending church to know how much to raise. A lack of robust financial policy is a loss of opportunity to educate church leaders on the needs of missionaries. On the opposite end of the spectrum, financial policies that are overly generous and lack convincing rationale will cause a church to feel frustrated that the bar is set so high or, even worse, that the agency is not prudent with finances and expect the church to simply come up with the money! An agency that adopts the *REMCAP* value of biblical centrality of the church will educate the church to take up its responsibility in the missionary enterprise, and will do so in a manner that respects the church's current abilities and values its sacrificial contribution.

The Church as Financial Supporters

The sending church is in the best position to raise the needed funds for the missionary. Such provision could come from the missions budget of a financially strong church, or the pastor could encourage the congregation to give. Such church support is extremely encouraging member care for missionaries. For example, a small church may not be able to increase the missions budget to provide for retirement needs, but when the pastor understands the issues and personally speaks on behalf of his missionary, people are much more likely to respond and the missionary would be immensely thankful. If pastors take the lead in raising support from their congregation for missionaries, then this brings care to an even higher level.

Supporting churches must be knowledgeable about the high financial cost of long-term missions involvement. Finances cannot be raised only for the field cost of living, but in the bigger long-term picture, we must consider children's education, retirement savings and fluctuating currencies in a global economy. Although pastors need not understand the technical intricacies of the finances of missions, they must be supportive of the personal budgets of the missionaries they send and value the agency's input to determine and monitor that budget. The backing of the pastor becomes even more critical when the missionary's budget is higher than the pastor's salary! The pastor must have a basic understanding of why this is so, and be able to explain it to the congregation.

When Michael and Jennifer's budgets were released, one church member questioned the missionary's total support budget because at first glance, it appeared to be more than the member's own salary. The pastor explained that the budget included ministry expenses and overseas travel, items that the missionary must raise, whereas these are "claimed" as work-related expenses in most companies. Other components were for retirement savings or children's education in an international school. When these items were explained and accounted for, the amount that the missionary received as "basic salary" was appropriate, and the church member appreciated that both the missionary was being provided for and the budgeting was prudent.

CMAT leaders agreed that if a missionary's support is coming from one primary sending church, then that church must have a greater role in querying and approving its missionary's budget. The church must decide on the level of support it will send, and this final decision may exclude some components that the agency recommends. Good practice in such a scenario is for the church to give its blessing to missionaries to raise this support from other donors. Mutual deference means that the church can hold its own policy and still allow the missionary to raise funds under the covering of the missions agency. Such practice acknowledges differences in policy while simultaneously valuing input from the agency and empowering the missionary.

CMAT leaders shared painful examples where churches forbade their missionaries to receive gifts for retirement or certain ministries, with the rationale that they were already being provided support from the church. A church leader asked a missions agency, "Do missionaries need annual leave or holidays?" Yet another church chose not to raise the financial support of its missionary for the past 20 years, citing the need to keep the missionary humble and dependant on the Lord as reasons. CMAT is strongly opposed to such regressive thinking.

In the past, this reasoning was applied to pastors, but we now correctly apply "you shall not muzzle an ox" and "the labourer deserves his wages" to pastors in full-time ministry (1 Tim 5:18). Even more so, we should accord the same honour and more to cross-cultural missionaries who sacrifice much and face many stressors in a challenging mission field (Rom 12:10). A sending church would be unwise to add further financial stress and pressure upon them.

The Missionary's Personal Responsibility

In addition to the instrumental roles played by the missions agency as an advocate and the sending church as a financial supporter, the missionary's personal role cannot be underestimated. Instead of waiting to be served and cared for, the missionary must be proactive and take initiative. He should be realistic and do all that he can and able as the Lord guides him. Fundraising efforts should not be seen as an unwelcome chore, but as part of the essential pre-field preparatory stage.

When considering additional needs, such as raising funds for retirement, a missionary should prayerfully find the right place, time and people to communicate the need. They can consider appointing someone as their financial coordinator, who acts as their communicator and facilitator in fundraising efforts. This relieves the missionary from having to attend to queries from his numerous supporters and frees him up to concentrate on the work of ministry.

Missionaries must be empowered to plan for their ministry and personal budgets, and to raise this financial support. Churches and missions agencies provide guidelines and accountability, but missionaries must take responsibility for their own financial well-being. Missionaries are not financially homogenous; a doctor in his forties who leaves his practice to go to the mission field is in a vastly different financial situation from a young adult planning for bible school and her first missions assignment. A church and agency's financial policies must treat both equitably. Thus, if one missionary has greater needs due to an insurance plan committed to when his salary was much higher, the church may rightfully choose not to support it, but should allow the missionary to raise these funds.

Tom and Mary were new missionaries who were delayed in being deployed to their field ministry because of insufficient financial support. They became increasingly discouraged and frustrated, as not enough people were supporting them. Their missions agency encouraged and guided them to deepen their spiritual maturity in this area. They used the two years of delay to build stronger rapport with leaders and members of their home church. They now look back on this delay as a test of faith that developed resilience and an essential part of their preparation for field ministry.

PARTNERSHIP ESSENTIALS

1. Long-term needs, such as retirement savings and home ownership, should be based on home country costs and built into a missionary's support budget.

2. The missions agency should provide flexible support levels to a missionary, such as minimal, basic and maximum amounts. On top of the basic amount, "good-to-have" items may be included in the budget, thus allowing the missionary to raise funds for them.

3. The sending church may choose to support the full missionary budget or less based on their missions policy, but should empower the missionary to raise finances for "good-to-have" items that the church is unable to provide for.

4. The church and missions agency will likely have different views on the amounts for the missionary. The greater the financially supporting role of the church, the more the agency should gladly submit to the church's view.

5. The good practice guidelines outlined by CMAT in this chapter serve as recommended positions that both churches and agencies can discuss and seek to align toward.

6. The missions agency's key partnership role in the area of finances is as an advocating educator. It educates both the missionary and church leaders on the financial cost of long-term missions, and advocates for the missionary's needs to financial supporters.

7. The church's key partnership role is as a financial supporter. Robust missions policy in the area of finances is a tremendous foundation for effective missionary care. Continual education of the congregation is essential for healthy, long-term support.

8. Missionaries must take personal responsibility and initiative for their own finances and fundraising. Instead of waiting to be served and cared for, they must take the initiative and receive empowerment not only for their basic needs but also for fundraising toward long-term savings.

9. No policy should be cast in stone. Both churches and agencies need to periodically evaluate their guidelines, whether on retirement savings, home components of support or other financial matters. Our world is changing faster than ever, with rapidly fluctuating national economies, increasing elderly populations and changing composition of congregations. When we hear of a good practice from another missions agency or church, or when a partner tells us that they are re-looking at their financial policies, let us take this not as a threat to our uneasy silence on the taboo of finances, but as opportunities to deepen our partnership and improve our own practices.

chapter 10

CONFLICT

Belinda Ng & Serene Lum

Sent by his Singapore church, Andrew, has been serving in Vietnam for more than ten years. During this time, he married Faith, a Filipino missionary whom his church leaders hardly knew. Their decision to continue supporting Andrew as a single missionary disappointed the couple. Over the years, a series of changes in missions pastors and missions policies at his home church had been stressful for him, and he was becoming increasingly frustrated that the church wanted more control over his ministry as he felt they were unfamiliar with the intricacies of his field.

After an open dialogue with the couple, the church leaders felt that Andrew wanted to be accountable first to the missions agency, then the church. The church leaders did not agree with this view, as they felt the church was sending Andrew and providing most of his funding. They also shared that, over the years, he had not been submissive to authority, and they perceived the couple was not being fruitful on the mission field. Andrew did not agree with their assessment, especially since he was in a pioneering ministry among an unreached people group. The sending relationship of more than ten years deteriorated to the point of tense discussion and confrontation.

The director of the missions agency listened to both sides and tried to facilitate a mutually agreeable Memorandum of Understanding (MOU). However, the church leaders and the missionaries could not reach an understanding. Andrew and Faith decided to resign from the church, but they remained with the missions agency on the field in Vietnam, with financial support raised through personal means from Singapore and sending support from Faith's church in the Philippines.

WITH PEOPLE COMES CONFLICT

Deteriorating relationships in missions partnerships cause great hurt to all the parties involved and often irreparable damage to the ministry. At times, conflict between the church and missions agency causes the missionary to be caught in the middle. In other instances, conflict within a missions team requires leaders to intervene. For Andrew and Faith, their declining relationship with their own church came to a painful end, with ties being severed between the missionary and church. Could there be better ways in managing such conflicts? Are there principles and values that church and agency leaders can uphold so that when inevitable issues surface, they can unite for a better outcome?

Conflict is a sharp disagreement in which the parties involved perceive a threat to their needs, interests or concerns. It can occur between two individuals, communities, groups, nations or organisations. Conflict happens when needs are unmet, or when a group or person is seen to be obstructing the goals of another group or person. As in the case above, Andrew perceived that his church wanted more control over his ministry, while the church leaders perceived that Andrew has been unfruitful in ministry and non-submissive to church authority, for he had married Faith, someone relatively unknown to them, without consultation.

No relationship is immune to conflict, but when managed biblically, conflict can serve as a catalyst for change, an opportunity for spiritual and relational growth, and a powerful testimony to the love and power of Jesus Christ. Scripture tells us that we are to "let all bitterness and wrath and anger and clamour and slander be put away from [us], along with all malice" (Eph 4:31). Failure to do so results in division in the body of Christ and grief to the Holy Spirit. We are also instructed not to allow a "root of bitterness" to spring up among us, leading to trouble and defilement (Heb 12:15). Learning how to deal with conflict is crucial, as opposed to avoidance or delay in dealing with it.

Interpersonal and inter-organisational conflicts are intertwined, and the biblical goal of conflict resolution is forgiveness and reconciliation. Christians are called to handle disputes in love, toward the hope of restoration. Interpersonal conflict needs to be handled in accordance to the principles in Matthew 18. This approach to conflict resolution is based on a desire for holy living and love for the person who has committed wrong.

Due to the church-agency partnership focus of this book, this chapter will not address the "how-to" of conflict resolution, but will instead surface pertinent issues in the tripartite relationship between the church, missions agency and missionary, and discuss how the *Relational Model of Church-Agency Partnerships (REMCAP)* may speak into these issues. We will consider factors that are essential in laying a solid foundation of trust and respect on which to build healthy partnerships that can withstand conflict when ministry goes awry.

GROWING APART FROM ONE ANOTHER

The deterioration of any longstanding relationship is particularly painful. In missions partnership, the distance and infrequency of communication increase the chances of growing apart from one another. When this occurs between the sending church and one of its own members after a decade on the field, the results are a heartrending reminder of the necessity of investing in the church-missionary relationship.

Changes Cause us to Grow Apart

Singapore's fast-changing environment leads to rapidly changing churches, and the church that a missionary was sent from ten years ago can be very different from the current church, even if leadership has not changed. When leadership, vision and policy changes take place, it becomes absolutely critical for the missionary to know and embrace what is occurring in his home church.

For Andrew, these changes in staffing and policies were understandably frustrating. Pastors assigned to missions may not be knowledgeable about their new responsibility, and less so about a particular field. While this can be frustrating for missionaries looking for knowledgeable support from their church, an alternative perspective for the missionaries in this situation is that part of their role is to inspire and educate their church in missions.

Though communication about the leadership and policy changes over the years did take place, unresolved tensions had built up over time and soured the church's relationship with Andrew. Churches should be mindful that changes in leadership, direction and policy are often extremely stressful to missionaries. If multiple major changes occur within the space of a few years, this is a particular warning that extra care must be given to good communication and the commitment of the relationship.

In this case, one of the changes that occurred on Andrew's side, not that of the church, was his decision to marry Faith. Some missions agencies have policies that guide such decisions, but even without such policies, the need to take time to discuss any major life change with one's leadership is evident, especially if that decision is cross-cultural marriage. Sending churches must be communicated with, missions agencies should be included, and the missionaries must be prepared for the increased complexities of two home fields, different home assignments and connecting with sending bodies in two countries. Unfortunately, Andrew's church leaders felt that they were not included in this process, bolstering their perception that he had made decisions on his own and lacked accountability. This perception would have only strengthened their desire to be kept informed and to institute guidelines stipulating that he must inform them of his field ministry decisions—moves that further alienated him.

Fruitfulness and Accountability to Church and Agency

In this case, the tensions arose because the missionary and church grew apart and were not able to restore a common understanding regarding accountability. The church was trying to uphold the value of biblical centrality of the church, but without the value of mutual deference in the key area of field accountability. The drafting of an MOU to address conflict in a time of crisis is difficult indeed. Achieving clarity is far easier when the problems are less severe, even better at the onset of the partnership. *REMCAP* helps by bringing a proven model that other churches and missions agencies also agree upon.

Concerns about accountability and fruitfulness are a common

occurrence in the tripartite church-agency-missionary relationship. While unease with lack of accountability can be addressed with clarity in reporting and communication, the concern about fruitfulness is one that varies significantly with ministry context. A large, successful church may have unspoken expectations that are not feasible for a frontier or pioneering missionary among an unreached people group. Open communication about the definition of fruitfulness that is specific to the context of the mission field would be valuable. What is very fruitful in one context may not be fruitful in another.

Losing the Sending Church

Church and Missions Agencies Together (CMAT) leaders were unanimous in agreement that a missionary without a sending church should not remain on the field. Even if a missionary has the resources to do so, remaining on the field with the agency contravenes the biblical centrality of the church. Ideally, missionaries who lose coverage of a sending church should spend time back in their home country establishing connections with another sending church. The time needed could vary from immediate to several years, depending on the depth of relationship acquired and policies of the new sending church. Since missionaries would eventually return to their home country, it is ideal that a sending church be identified in their home country.

Increasing complexities abound in this case and in our environment today. First, it is increasingly common for Singaporean churches to send missionaries of other nationalities. In such a scenario, it is preferable, for example, that a sending church in Indonesia be identified for an Indonesian missionary, so that the Singaporean church can jointly send the missionary with the Indonesian church.

While the arrangements are more complex and difficult at first, the benefit to the missionaries is that they have a sending church in their home country to handle certain missionary care needs, such as care of the missionaries' families and transitions after the field.

For Andrew and Faith, they also had a church in the Philippines, which was Faith's sending church. Thus, they could remain on the field in partnership with that church. However, it would be wise for the agency to advise Andrew to form a relationship with another church in Singapore that could provide some care in his home country.

MAINTAINING PARTNERSHIPS AMIDST CONFLICT

Just as in marriage, missions partnerships inevitably involve conflict at some point in time. Therefore, at the onset of a partnership, a partnership model like *REMCAP* and strong commitment to the relationship will help to minimise the number of conflicts that may arise and maintain partnerships in the midst of the inevitable conflicts that we all must deal with.

The partnership values in *REMCAP* provide a framework for the conduct of the partnership and a mutual understanding that helps partners strengthen relationships and facilitate conflict resolution. Such a framework guides churches and agencies in the difficult times of conflict that will inevitably surface later. The values form the foundation, while the rest of the model describes the roles and decision-making responsibilities of either the church or agency. If a tripartite partnership between the church, agency and missionary discusses and honours the biblical centrality of the church, accords each entity equal value, and works together with glad submission and mutual deference in joyful fellowship, then the foundation for successful partnership conflict resolution would be firmly laid.

Goodwill Trust and Competence Trust

We all know that trust is essential in any relationship and extremely fragile in times of conflict. In Christian partnerships, we are sometimes too quick to assume trust, saying that we trust one another, because we do not doubt a person's moral character. However, trust in partnerships consists of more than one component and does not only relate to a person's integrity. Understanding the distinction between the two types of trust— goodwill trust and competence trust—can help us further understand how the *REMCAP* partnership values guide us to establish a strong base of trust that can withstand conflict (Das and Teng 255–58).

Goodwill trust is that kind of trust that we often first think of when we ask ourselves whether we trust someone. It refers to a partner's intentions to perform his side of the partnership and is related to issues of morality, integrity, responsibility and dependability. When Duane Elmer writes, "Trust is the ability to build confidence in a relationship so that both parties believe the other will not intentionally hurt them but will act in their best interest," he is talking about goodwill trust (77). When we practice the value of joyful fellowship and encouragement, we are building goodwill trust that becomes a tremendous strength when conflicts arise. A high level of goodwill trust due to joyful fellowship is a great strength in difficult times of conflict.

At the beginning of a new church-agency relationship we do not typically doubt another person's morality or integrity, but if expectations are repeatedly not met and agreements are not honoured, we will begin to doubt the person or organisation's responsibility and dependability. Perhaps they intended to fulfil their part of the partnership at first, but they are not doing it now. Goodwill trust is eroded as we perceive the other is less reliable, even if we do not think they are acting deceptively. The hurt they are causing may not be intentional, but we stop believing they are acting in our best interests.

This erosion may occur if church leaders question a missionary's fruitfulness on the field, or if an agency thinks church leaders are interfering too much with field decisions and ministry. When we recognise that goodwill trust is decreasing in a relationship, we can address it by openly admitting that this is detracting from our equal value of one another. We can begin to restore this when we understand the problem from the other person or organisations' perspective. Understanding behaviour from the viewpoint of another and acknowledging their limitations help us to restore goodwill trust and to put measures in place that are acceptable to all parties.

Competence trust is another kind of trust where one believes that partners have the ability, skills, knowledge and experience to fulfil their responsibilities in the partnership. Whereas goodwill trust is usually high at the beginning of a partnership, this is often not the case with competence trust. Large churches sometimes doubt the contribution of smaller missions agencies, or an inexperienced pastor may take up missions leadership responsibilities to the concern of missionaries and agency leaders. When we meet potential partners, we often assess their competence to fulfil their side of the relationship and ask ourselves, "Can I trust this person's or organisation's competence to perform?"

Low competence trust can sometimes be dealt with by sharing experiences and assuring others that the organisation can handle a situation. An agency director may talk about the specialist resources that the agency has, thus reassuring the church. At other times, only longer periods of training or experience may sufficiently equip an inexperienced leader to the point where competence trust is no longer an issue. In such cases, low competence trust can be managed by bolstering up other areas. For example, a new leader may not have the competence to handle the missionaries and the array of challenges under his care, so more guidance and frequent feedback from an experienced coach would help him personally. Reviewing the mutual expectations within an MOU would also help all parties gain clarity and acknowledge results and progress in specific areas, thus maintaining the relationship even though competence trust is low.

Glad Submission and Mutual Deference

Whenever different opinions surface, the importance of the value of glad submission and mutual deference becomes increasingly apparent. Conflict arises when submission is grudging or deference is not mutual; thus, internalisation of this value and its practice would result in partners willingly looking for opportunities to model the Trinitarian relationship by deferring and submitting gladly to one another, thus averting many conflicts.

When conflict has already risen, partners can return to this value and consider how Scripture calls us to respond. *REMCAP* provides good practice guidelines on the specific areas that should primarily be the church's responsibility and those that should belong to the agency, according to the distinction—"church family at home" and "agency family at work". Discussing the application of these guidelines can show the way forward in many conflict scenarios that recur on the mission field and in our partnerships.

Constant Communication

At the beginning of a partnership, an MOU may facilitate this communication by establishing healthy expectations. A sending church may sometimes be unsure of its role and not feel a positive sense of ownership of the ministry. Sharing of information by the agency honours the biblical centrality of the church—creating greater understanding of issues, mutual accountability in the ministry, and the respective roles of the church and agency.

During a sending partnership, difficult situations that increase tension and the probability of conflict will inevitably arise. A project may fail or differing views on strategy may surface. At these times, both the church and agency must make additional effort to share information and communicate with one other during this difficult period. The agency and church each has valuable knowledge in their respective spheres, with the agency majoring in field matters and the church in the supporting constituency of the missionary. Challenging situations often require input from both sides—the home front and the field. Equal value of each other means valuing these contributions, both in times of tension and direct conflict.

Communication is also particularly needed when significant changes occur on either side of the partnership. A change in person responsible for leadership may occur when a new missions pastor is hired by the church, or there is a change in agency director. Sometimes, policy changes are implemented, resulting in sudden changes in finances or home assignment expectations. At other times, organisational culture and guidelines may gradually change over time. Such changes may evidence themselves as shifts in missions direction, missionary expectation, or even placement in certain countries or ministries.

Life changes in a missionary such as marriage or new births require increased communication between leaders and missionaries. For example, marriage and children significantly affect financial support-raising guidelines, especially if the marriage is a cross-cultural union. Other life changes, such as children progressing to university studies or, in the case of Singapore, male children returning to Singapore for compulsory National Service, require communication between the church, agency and missionary regarding expectations and finances, otherwise conflict is more likely to arise.

Positive and Preventative Measures

In the face of challenging ministry, emotional stressors and the reality of spiritual warfare, the church and agency need to have in place positive measures that help prevent conflict from escalating and build relational capital, which is invaluable when conflict does arise.

Regular debriefs during home assignments is one way of recognising and addressing conflict through regular check-ups. While agencies typically conduct such debriefs, the church can also conduct its own debrief to hear from its missionary. When leaders sense a possibility of conflict, having a neutral and safe party who can debrief the missionary would be preferable. Processing of field experiences in a safe and confidential environment will facilitate the uncovering of any tense issues, which can then be dealt with before they escalate.

When a church is actively engaged in a missionary's ministry, this involvement builds bonds that can withstand the stress of conflict. Church leaders must take the initiative for these opportunities, such as scheduling missionaries to share about their ministries with church members in worship services, seminars or prayer meetings. Sending missions teams to work alongside missionaries, providing time and finances for rest and renewal, as well as resourcing missionaries for personal development and skills upgrading, are all ways of building trust and deeper involvement in the lives of missionaries. In short, any type of member care that is valued by a missionary, especially those listed in *REMCAP* under "church family at home" and "agency family at work", will build strong bonds that can weather the storms of conflict. With strong ties, it is unlikely that missionaries would desire to end their relationships with a sending church.

MANAGING CONFLICT FROM A DISTANCE

One unique aspect of conflict in a missions setting is that the conflict is often managed from a distance. While this remote situation is not ideal, it is often a necessary reality. In particular, conflicts often occur on the field between team members, while the church and the home side of the missions agency are thousands of kilometres away in the sending country. Though field leadership may be present, those leaders may themselves be embroiled in the conflict. Even when field leadership is neutral and available to manage the conflict, the church and agency at home still have valuable roles to play.

Care and Resolution

In this case of conflict on the field, the agency has the first responsibility to address the matter and resolve the conflict. The home director would have greater knowledge of the field structures and process used by the agency in dealing with the conflict. The agency's responsibility is thus resolving the conflict while guiding and caring for the missionaries involved. Conflict may occur between two missionaries from the same missions agency and team; thus, the agency may also be responsible for correction, counselling or discipline.

The church's responsibility is different in that it focuses on caring for its missionary. The church should be mindful to not interfere in the resolution process that the agency has put in place. In another case study discussed by CMAT, a church was concerned for its missionaries after conflict in their team steadily increased over several years. They were careful not to interfere with agency decisions and processes at first, only stepping in after a long period when it felt that its missionaries were being unfairly treated. Strong communication between the agency director and church leaders resulted in the tense situation turning out well.

In a sense, the church's role in field conflict is simpler than that of the agency, since it focuses on the caring and not the resolution. However, the church must also deal with the flow of information to and from the congregation, as the missionary has relationships through the church, not only with the leaders. Sometimes this flow is helpful in that members of the congregation who are personally on close terms with the missionary may alert church leaders to tense issues while they are still manageable. Such positive relationships are built when leaders encourage regular church members to visit missionaries and communicate regularly with them. At other times, when conflict has already escalated to a crisis, information flow to the congregation becomes a complexity that must be managed until the church and agency leaders can make the necessary decisions.

Seeking Reconciliation

In cases like Andrew and Faith's situation, a conflict may occur between the missionary and either the agency or church leaders at home. In conflict situations, communication has most likely already broken down, so the distance between the missionary and home becomes another hurdle to cross. Videoconferencing technologies, such as Skype and FaceTime, are helpful but not a substitute for "real-life" personal interaction. In such situations, church and agency leaders must take the initiative to meet face to face, by either flying to the mission field or buying an air-ticket for the missionary to return home to work through the conflict.

In all conflicts, reconciliation is always the goal that we must seek. However, in Singapore—as in many shame and honour cultures— open dialogue and confrontation of issues are not common practices. Thus, when a conflict arises, it is more likely than not that the matter has already been festering for too long. Thus, the reconciliation process often involves working through the pain and stress that are hurting the parties involved and threatening the work of ministry. For these reasons, the effort required is significant, but it is well worth it. Reconciliation is vital for growth and maturity in God's kingdom, whether that occurs in the life of the missionary, the church or the agency.

PARTNERSHIP ESSENTIALS

1. Church and missions agency leaders will inevitability handle some form of conflict in their sending partnership. The manner in which leaders manage this conflict will have a huge impact on the potential restoration of relationship and ministry on the field.

2. Strengthen goodwill trust and competence trust in the partnership. Don't assume trust just because we do not doubt

moral character. Rebuild goodwill trust when it is weakened by unmet expectations, discuss shortcomings and implement measures to strengthen trust in each other's competence. Equally value each organisation's unique contributions.

3. Look for opportunities to practice glad submission and mutual deference. We have internalised this value when occasions to submit and defer are viewed as ways to honour the Godhead in our relationships.

4. Constantly communicate, especially in times of change or tension, or when there is a risk of conflict. Partners can feel slighted and used when decisions are made or events occur without their knowledge, so resolve misunderstandings quickly. Communication is particularly needed when changes occur in policy, strategy or people in leadership.

5. Care for missionaries in ways they value the most from the church as family at home and the agency as family at work. Build positive relationship capital, which reduces the chance of conflict occurring and withstands the pressures of inevitable conflict that arises.

6. Conflict is best handled closest to the place of occurrence, but management from a distance is sometimes unavoidably necessary, especially when conflict occurs on the field.

7. The agency's primary responsibility is to resolve the conflict in ways that build up and protect the missionaries involved. The church's responsibility is to care for its missionary and be careful not to unduly interfere with the process of resolution.

Open communication between church and agency leaders would ensure that understanding occurs without a sense of interference. Further, when a worker is aware that his church and agency are actively communicating and working together, good resolution is much more likely to take place.

8. Reconciliation must be the goal for believers in conflict. Every church-agency-missionary partnership is valuable, and Christ's desire is for conflict to be resolved within the body, such that our relationships reflect the Trinitarian relationship (Jn 17). Jesus teaches us to "first be reconciled to your brother and then come and offer your gift" of worship. Thus, we are called to deal with problems in our partnership openly, honestly and humbly—whether the conflict occurs on the field within a team, between missionaries and church leaders, or between church and agency leaders.

chapter 11

CRISIS MANAGEMENT

Brent Lindquist & Daphne Teo

Global Outreach Church had numerous missionary units on the mission field in the Philippines. These included a single man, woman and two families with young children. Additionally, one family had a child with special medical needs that required constant electrical and electronic monitoring.

A typhoon swept through causing widespread destruction. Relief efforts were underway, but a disease outbreak threatened further loss of life to everyone involved, including the missionaries. Multiple agencies and churches had missionaries on this field, all with varying concerns.

Global Outreach Church had its own deliberations and decided to recall all its missionaries from the field, citing concerns for their safety. It came to this decision unilaterally, without consultation from the field or missions agency director. The church communicated this decision to the missionaries and agency director, and gave instructions for its missionaries to return home.

The family with the special needs child, who had been taking the lead in demanding that they return home immediately, was relieved. The other missionaries, however, were frustrated because they had already been working on relief issues, even taking on coordinating roles within the multi-mission response task force.

Further, this caused disruption over the whole region, as many families became anxious over whether their own board and church might also follow suit to summon them home.

UNPREPARED FOR CRISES

When things are going well, the church and missions agency typically do not worry too much about details. It takes a major crisis to upset this easy-going relationship, particularly when lives are apparently at stake.

Too often, church missions policy guidelines are vague about crisis management, if such guidelines exist at all. The unspoken assumption is that things will not go wrong, or won't go terribly wrong. Sadly, things do go wrong, and then leaders scramble to understand the situation and how to care for all involved.

This struggle of not pre-emptively preparing for crises is partly related to a lack of understanding of the different kinds of crises that missionaries experience. In this chapter, we will refer to the following definitions and types of crises: personal or family, trauma, armed conflict and complex humanitarian emergency.

A personal or family crisis is one that happens to the missionaries themselves, their family on the field or their family members back home. An example might be someone getting sick, injured or killed through an accident that involves only that person or a small entity, such as a missionary being involved in an automobile accident that requires medical and/or legal attention.

A trauma crisis is one in which the missionaries or their families are traumatised by an event. This could include being robbed, threatened, raped or in a situation that causes harm to them.

An armed conflict could include missionaries getting involved in the surrounding political problems such as demonstrations, terrorist attacks and the like. These are often quite complex and not isolated instances. For example, there are parts of the world where on-going conflicts have existed for years.

A complex humanitarian emergency would be a complicated and long emergency or trauma, such as an earthquake or tsunami, and its aftermath. This could go on for years, requiring a completely new philosophy of ministry, relocation and other things.

DIFFERENT TYPES OF CRISES

Each type of crisis requires a different set of responses on the part of the church and mission agency. The appropriate response can make the difference between comfort or confusion, between making the situation better or worse. Applying the right responses can be difficult. Other governmental agencies may be involved and legal consequences may complicate the situation. For example, a missionary involved in a car accident in some countries may be jailed until the issue is resolved in court, regardless of whether the accident was his fault or not.

While every crisis situation is unique and we cannot predict every possibility, understanding the common factors involved in the different types of crises will help the church and missions agency prepare for the time when a crisis does occur.

Personal or Family Crisis

This kind of crisis may be easier to manage than other crises, in that having the missionary family come home may be the most important decision to be made. However, these simple issues sometimes fall through the cracks because the missions agency needs to keep the coordinator connected to both the missionary and the mission. If the missionary comes home due to a medical issue, then there may be a need for extra coordination for the insurance programme. If the return is due to a mental health or moral issue, then some personnel decisions, which may have consequences, will have to be made. All the involved parties need to have regular communication with each other. In the case of a health crisis, the missionary needs to be the responsible party, depending on confidentiality regulations.

Trauma and Armed Conflict

These types of crises are more complex because legal issues may be present and legal authorities may be involved. It is very important that the mission understands the legal climate of the country. How and when are complaints made? Does the mission have access to attorneys who can help? What if incarceration is a possibility? This chapter cannot address all of these scenarios, but it is important for the church to ask the mission how it handles these situations.

In the best case, the missions agency has guidelines in place for each scenario. The church can review the guidelines with the missions agency liaison. Once the guidelines are understood, the church can then ask the missions agency how the agency can help as the crisis progresses. Such crises sometimes require high degrees of confidentiality as negotiations go on, and it is easy for the church to feel left out. If that happens, the church leaders should always express their feelings. Perhaps, a church staff member could be allowed to be made aware of certain issues as long as they are kept confidential. However, the reality is that the larger the circle, the easier it is for information to be leaked, which could lead to extremely negative outcomes.

Complex Humanitarian Emergency

By definition, a complex humanitarian emergency is chronic, chaotic and long term. An earthquake can have geological aftershocks for months, and the emotional aftershocks can go on for years. This will undoubtedly require a different level of involvement on the field by both the mission and church, with the potential for long-term change of missions strategy due to the emergency.

MANAGING A CRISIS TOGETHER

The case study presented earlier is a complex humanitarian emergency where the church made a unilateral decision and informed the missions agency. Dealing with a crisis situation is becoming increasingly common, whether the crisis is political, an act of terrorism, a natural disaster or a disease epidemic. In these situations, it is crucial that the decision-making process involves all parties.

Field Leadership, not Unilateral Decisions

If one party feels that a decision is unilateral, then this is a key indicator that such an action is damaging to the relationship. Often, such actions leave people feeling unhappy and may even hinder future ministry. Biblical centrality of the church does not mean that unilateral decisions should be made by the church. Certainly, the church must be involved, but it should defer to the missionary and missions agency because local information near to the source is the most valuable.

News reports received via the media and the Internet often make a crisis look more critical than it really is. For instance, a bomb blast may be perceived by the sending church as a critical crisis, whereas the missionary may not view himself to be in any immediate danger, as the blast happened in another neighbourhood. Therefore, the church should defer to those with local knowledge on the field. The ultimate decision on whether to evacuate or not may lie with the area leader, country leader or team leader, depending on the structure of the missions agency.

National partners are often not only a valuable source of information, but also an invaluable asset in consultation. Often, we think that local believers will feel abandoned if foreign missionaries evacuate during a crisis. This may sometimes be the case, for there are reports that ministry has had breakthroughs when missionaries stay amidst crisis. On the other hand, there have been accounts of locals advising missionaries, "You should leave now while you can. You are in more danger than we are, and if you stay, you will put us at greater risk!"

Pressure and Prudence

The missions agency should keep in mind, however, that the church often faces pressure from family members and the congregation who are worried about their missionary. The church may want to bring the missionary home, believing that it is the best way to extend missionary care. The church leadership may also feel that prudence is the best option, as they would have to bear the fallout if something negative—which they could have prevented—happens to their missionary.

The role of the missionaries and how they facilitate this process is critical. As they are simultaneously communicating with their family, church and agency leaders, they should wisely manage the communication, in particular the feelings of their family members and church community who are geographically removed from the crisis and may be thinking the worst.

Information Flow

Guarding information flow due to the sensitivities surrounding an armed conflict or trauma is crucial. In the case of a missionary being injured or worse, it would be unfortunate if the information communicated to the church or supporters found its way to the news media, because it could endanger the missionary on the field. An analogy is a rape victim who has received threats—if the home church or supporters accidently communicated this information to the news media, in such manner that the victim is identified or the hospital where the victim is being treated is named, then there is a great risk of the perpetrators locating and harming the victim.

In the case of an armed conflict, there are similar issues to be cautious about. For example, in a particular military coup, missionaries were asked by reporters to comment for the news cameras. Although they were not authorised by their missions agency to speak, they went ahead thinking that they had taken sufficient precautions. As a result, they inadvertently disclosed information that compromised their location and safety.

Preplanning

It is of strategic value that extensive preplanning be done with the church and agency about how crises are understood, and in the case of terrorism or political events, which external references would be the thought leaders. For instance, for US agencies, the State Department or the Homeland Security may become the reference points in determining evacuation. In Singapore, the Ministry for Foreign Affairs guides in crises and evacuation scenarios.

The missions agency needs to have ready-to-implement evacuation models, which may include restrictions in daily activities, and differing levels of evacuation preparedness. For each emergency, there needs to exist clear and continuous contact with a Crisis Management Team (CMT), which may be managed by the agency but is also easily accessible to the church. Family anxieties will compound and cloud decision-making in difficult times; therefore, it may be necessary to have a way to reinstitute a plan if the original falls apart.

For example, a church may agree beforehand to consult with the mission in times of crisis, but then acts unilaterally to bring its missionaries home. Realising this may happen, there should be a "Plan B" in place to help care for the missionaries regardless of whether they are evacuated. We need to avoid finger pointing and focus on caring for our people.

ROLES & RESPONSIBILITIES

In the middle of a crisis, a commander who can take charge of the situation is needed. Due to its wealth of data on the field and intelligence and experience in this area, the missions agency needs to be in charge and to manage triage, while the church can contribute to follow-up pastoral care. This care may apply when the missionary is feeling stress on the field, but is especially needed if evacuation to the home country occurs. In the best possible scenario, both the church and agency should work together under the leadership of the missions agency's CMT to make decisions regarding the crisis. Communication avenues should be specified ahead of time, including contact people at the church and missions agency, and substitutes in case the main person is not accessible.

The Missions Agency Leads from the Field

It is important for the missionaries' own sense of stability and security to know who is responsible for them while they are on the field. By virtue of the missions agency having the staff and experience in managing crises on the field, it needs to continue to lead from the field as the primary entity. This does not mean that the affected missionary is making decisions, but rather that the missions agency's CMT leads from the field and makes decisions in consultation with the others, for they are in the best position to know and understand all the information about the crisis. In the best of circumstances, information needs to flow to the missions agency first, and from the agency to the church and family members.

However, in real life, this does not always happen. A crisis may occur on a weekend, for example, and the missionary calls his family back home first. Missions agencies sometimes find out about a crisis after the family and church have been alerted. Agencies generally find it difficult to take leadership after other stakeholders have already been involved. Sometimes, they are already attempting to travel to the place of crisis. There should be an agreement stating that whoever hears about a crisis first must always inform the missions agency, for the CMT to make decisions and take action.

This arrangement can be practically worked out between the local church and missions agency by talking through some practice scenarios. While no one can predict everything that could happen, having a broad understanding of strategies and concepts, as outlined in this chapter, can help mitigate unavoidable stress or conflict.

The Church Family Ministers in Crisis

Based on the above, a church may feel like they are being placed in a secondary role in a crisis response situation. To a certain extent, this is true in initial stages of crisis, for the missions agency needs to develop the crisis management strategy. To complement the agency, the church would be most effective focusing on responsive strategies of care as opposed to initiating strategies of care. Once the mission has stabilised the circumstances and a plan of action has been developed, the church could become involved, typically at home but even on the field if that is part of the plan.

The church is especially suited to step in to provide care if the missionary needs to return home. The church family can take over the coordination and provision of care so that the missions agency can release more resources back to the field-based crisis. Partnership in this manner allows for integrated care for the missionary. Consultation between the church and agency is needed for status updates, provision of counselling and additional costs incurred.

Even if the missionary does not return home, pastoral care from the church is invaluable in times of crisis. This care could include gathering information about the particular needs of the family, prayer items that can be shared among the people gathering for prayer in the church, and strategies and resources to be given to the missionary family once they arrive home. In cases where the family remains on the field for an extended period of time, the church could work with the missions agency regarding visitation and sending of resources.

In a comprehensive or complex humanitarian emergency such as an earthquake, the missions agency may need to consider and implement significant changes in ministry strategy. The church's role would involve giving input, and being understanding and supportive of this change. For example, in the Global Outreach Church case study presented earlier, one of the missionary families became deeply involved in relief and development after the typhoon. They did not want to be evacuated, but felt pressured by the church to do so, as their leaders did not share their passion for the ministry strategy that was developing. Church and agency leaders who are sending missionaries to areas where complex humanitarian emergencies occur frequently should prepare for such scenarios before they occur.

CRISIS MANAGEMENT PROTOCOL

Having a known course of action and process of decision-making helps the missions agency and sending church to manage crises when they occur. A crisis management protocol helps us prepare for a crisis, think through the multiple factors involved in handling a crisis and deal with them adequately. Such guidelines are especially helpful in managing information flow and communication with all involved parties. Clear and regular communication helps avoid misunderstanding and prevent secondary crisis situation from arising due to miscommunication.

Crisis Management Team

A CMT should be appointed within the organisations to be trained in crisis management. Members of the CMT should undergo training and drills, which would include risk assessment and evaluation, policy execution and communications.

A missions agency and church will have their own CMT that reflects their own structure of leadership and communication. Each CMT knows its protocol in relation to its own organisation and to one another in the church-agency partnership. Disruption to regular office operations is thereby minimised while managing the crisis. Engaging in proactive planning will help facilitate wise stewardship of resources (money, time and personnel).

Scope and Principles

The crisis protocol encompasses the immediate response during and shortly after the crisis. It does not deal with long-term care subsequent to the crisis. It is a tool to help agencies and churches to manage the details. Top level leadership must assess the needs and consider the ramifications of specific actions before implementing them. CMAT adopts the following principles in our crisis response protocols for our respective churches and missions agencies.

1. The church and missions agency equally value one another in the crisis response, with close communication throughout the crisis. The church defers to the missions agency's CMT leadership, especially in the immediate response and decisions for the crisis.

2. The crisis protocol must reflect the organisation's values, such that these values help to shape the crisis response. Procedures help leaders take action with beneficial strategies that keep people safe, and contribute to them thriving, not merely surviving.

3. God is in control, and a biblical perspective on the crisis is essential. Prayer during a crisis period is crucial, but a balance of managing information flow and mobilising prayer simultaneously is needed.

4. Though we aim to minimise damage to our personnel on the field, our actions must also take into consideration the potential impact on the nationals whom we serve.

5. The missions agency's CMT needs to communicate appropriate decisions to the parties concerned. The church's CMT should communicate their concerns back to the missions agency's CMT and the field leadership. Depending on the crisis and pre-existing relationships, either the agency's or church's CMT may communicate with the family members on the home side.

6. The missions agency's CMT may also need to consider how to work with both the local and home governments and other NGOs to assist their missionaries more effectively through the crisis.

7. Diverse views and opinions are inevitable, especially in complex crises. The goal of a wise and unified leadership response is achievable with the CMAT values of equal value, glad submission and mutual deference. Such a response is greatly facilitated when pre-existing positive relationships between the church and missions agency leadership have been developed.

Immediate Response

The flow of response describes how a CMT first learns about and takes action in the event of a crisis:

1. Crisis onset. News of a developing crisis could come from a call from the field, warnings from partner organisations, or Ministry of Foreign Affairs or news reports.

2. Gather as much information as possible. Make sure you can maintain contact with the information source. Verify information with other sources. Establish details regarding the personnel affected, the area affected by the crisis and the prognosis of the crisis.

3. Control information. Request the information source to halt the flow of news until the church and/or agency is able to formulate a response. Only the appointed official spokesperson should communicate with the media.

   • Organisational leaders decide whether or not to activate the CMT. The leader or CMT then decides who to inform about the crisis and appoints a person to handle communications.

   • Staff are reminded to keep confidentiality and to give the official organisational response. Decide how to handle information circulating from other sources.

   • Give regular updates to the appropriate parties according to a previously developed plan. Provide consistent news to churches, families, boards and prayer networks.

4. Start a log. Record everything about the crisis. Create a log of decisions made, actions taken and communications completed. These include dates and times, phone calls with brief descriptions and minutes of meetings.

5. Facilitate finances. Expedite funds for missionaries to handle the crisis. Assess what funds are needed and available. Acquire necessary approvals quickly. Assist in

insurance claims if missionaries require medical attention in the home country.

6. Develop an initial missionary care plan. Determine the urgent and important needs. Call missionaries on the field to encourage and assure them. Visit families of missionaries, if needed. Prepare to receive evacuees with accommodation and hospitality. Brief agency staff and church members on appropriate reception. Provide medical or counselling assistance now, or at a later stage if more appropriate.

After the Crisis

When the crisis is over, the CMT's response and communication should be evaluated. Strategies can then be affirmed or refined. Depending on the nature of the crisis, an after-care plan may be needed. The original CMT from the respective churches and agencies would not be the best group to handle this, as the needs are primarily member care-related. Therefore, a post-CMT that consists of member care staff from the missions agency and church leaders can ensure that missionaries are getting the care and treatment they need.

Both the church and missions agency should be involved in planning and meeting the member care needs of the missionary. While the missions agency's role is primary during the immediate onset of a crisis, the longer the crisis continues, especially if a missionary returns home for a period, the more the church's role is needed to help its members settle back at home and in ministry, even if only for a few weeks or months. Therefore, a strong partnership between the church and agency to support missionaries and their families in crisis is essential.

PARTNERSHIP ESSENTIALS

1. Crises are an unavoidable eventuality in missions partnerships. They can take the form of a personal or family crisis, traumatic event, armed conflict or complex humanitarian emergency.

2. Crisis management best occurs in partnership, with clear lines of communication, responsibility and decision-making among the church, agency and missionary.

3. The church and missions agency will value one another and not make unilateral decisions, for these wreak havoc on not only the partnership, but also the missionaries and their ministries.

4. The missions agency leads from the field, for it is in the best place to gather information from the field and make decisions. The church defers initial decisions regarding immediate response, such as potential evacuation and triage, to the missions agency.

5. The church ministers to missionaries in crises, taking on an increasingly important missionary care role as the crisis extends, especially if the missionary returns home.

6. A crisis management protocol that addresses both the agency and church roles is an invaluable tool in the event of an emergency. A pre-emptively trained CMT will handle decisions and the complex flow of information to stakeholders.

7. Crisis management protocols must be reviewed regularly because crises do not occur on schedule, leaders change position, and new staff may only be aware of the protocol theoretically.

part 3

IMPACTING PARTNERSHIPS AROUND YOU

chapter 12

STARTING YOUR OWN CMAT

Ivan Liew

Halfway through a long-distance bike ride, I dream of the finish line and the hot shower awaiting me. Nearing the end of my research studies, I dreamed of the formation of the first group of churches and missions agencies who would meet to take the work further than I could on my own. Finally, when this group became a team, we dreamed of the completion of this book.

Now you, the reader, have this material in your hands. You and I are nearing the end of our journey together. Churches and Missions Agencies Together (CMAT) has shared our research and model with you. The rigour of our discussions has been imperfectly translated into a guide of good practice, which we hope that others will find beneficial. It is not perfect, but we hope that it will stir discussion, encourage communication and improve partnerships among other missions leaders.

I would like to invite you to dream one step further. Would you consider starting your own group of CMAT? The first pilot working group purposely gave ourselves this generic yet descriptive name "CMAT" so that it could also describe other groups. We never wanted to be the only exclusive. We hope that you can start your own CMAT within your own church-agency relationships.

TOO GOOD TO KEEP TO OURSELVES

For this reason, we believe that the process that our first CMAT group went through is even more fundamental than the guidelines presented in Part 2 of this book. Like good news that is too beneficial to keep to ourselves, we want to share the experiences that had strengthened our own partnerships. While elements in the process have been mentioned in Chapter 5, this chapter is dedicated to describing the steps that will help you to be a part of something similar.

Important Improvements

Why is starting a group like CMAT important for you? I am not talking about why church-agency partnerships are important, as I would be preaching to the choir. More specifically, I am asking why improving the way we practise our partnership between church and missions agency is so important.

First, we missions leaders know that our own church-agency partnership practice can be greatly improved, yet we do not talk about it openly and so struggle to improve it. I have had people tell me they are thankful for their partnerships, but have never met anyone who tells me they are confident about their partnerships or that they have a strong grasp or understanding on how to work out church-agency partnership matters. Instead, when I share examples of uncertainties, struggles and unspoken tensions between churches and agencies, I always get knowing nods indicating, "Yes, I've seen that and feel that, too!"

In contrast, I have met many people who are confident in other areas of ministry. We have leadership experts, preaching giants and missiological geniuses. However, the global Church does not have a strong body of data that exists about how church-agency partnerships are conducted that others could learn from. I have benefitted from good articles on church-agency partnerships and strong papers on church and parachurch relations written by theologians, but very few resources exist compared to other missions areas. In particular, I am not aware of a book or peer-reviewed research that has dealt with the topic of how to manage our church-agency partnerships, despite acknowledgements that this is a critical area in need of improvement.

The second reason for improving church-agency partnership practice is that, in our conversations with one another in the pilot CMAT and with other agency and church leaders, we hear of the same ministry struggles that recur over and over again. Some of these afflictions are a necessary part of ministry, and we rejoice to be counted worthy to suffer in this manner. However, many instances of pain are unnecessarily inflicted upon one another and the missionaries we send because of ineffective partnership practices.

The same mistakes are being repeated by different church and agency leaders in different denominations and sending nations. By learning to improve partnerships in community with one another and sharing our knowledge, we build a body of data that will be of great practical help to the churches and missions agencies after us.

Finally, and by no means the least important, we improve the way we relate to one other because this is glorifying to God. My firm belief is that, in addition to interpersonal relationships, inter-organisational relationships glorify God when they display the unity of the global Church. We, who have been created in the image of God, have also been given the image of the Trinitarian relationships on which to model our relationships in order that the world may believe in Christ's message through us (Jn 17:20-21). If we admit that our partnerships do not display the unity within the body of Christ that we should, then we should make an effort to improve our partnerships, so that they are worthy of the gospel we proclaim (Php 1:27).

Needful yet Neglected

Like a neglected child in the missiological family, the "how to" of improving church-agency partnership practice has not received much attention. Without a strong body of agreed-upon evidence, efforts to improve partnerships have often been a mixture of well-meaning personal efforts that have not resulted in much-needed wider and stronger resonance.

Missions agency leaders often want to improve partnerships, but find it difficult to engage meaningfully with church leaders, even though that they recognise this is a central part of their ministry. Some church leaders are not aware of the importance of their role in missions-sending. They love their missionaries but lack the love-language to communicate this care. While the growing prevalence of member care as a professional and clinical specialty has contributed to good practice, the corresponding meagre discussion about the church's role in member care only serves to reinforce the unspoken and erroneous idea in many churches that their missions role is secondary and not so important.

Even when churches desire to be involved more extensively in missions, other unspoken tensions arise. Agencies worry, "Perhaps the church board will be too controlling. They mean well but will interfere and don't understand the field context." In Singapore, these tensions are known but not typically expressed out loud. Thus, the very need for improving church-agency partnerships becomes the reason for its neglect.

Finally, another reason for neglecting what is important is that we do not know what to do about it. New partnerships are a wonderful time to talk about structures and expectations of the church and agency. However, after the practical matters are settled, these discussions do not go deeper, because we do not have a framework for church-agency partnerships. For the organisation that does have a policy of church-agency partnerships, it is typically written from the perspective of that agency or church, and is therefore not a shared framework for improving partnerships. Amidst the urgent matters of ministry, the important but non-urgent matter of improving church-agency partnerships is often left undone.

Making a Difference

The research, model and processes described in this book can address the reasons for neglecting this important matter of our church-agency partnership. The *Relational Model of Church-Agency Partnerships (REMCAP)* describes the constitutive ingredients of these relationships and how they work in Chapters 4-5. With greater understanding, we know where to focus to improve what we are doing. We have values to guide us, and in Chapters 6–11, we expounded on six foundational issues in church-agency partnership.

While we still lack a broad body of evidence regarding church-agency partnership practice, we have a solid start with the churches and agencies represented in this book. As more leaders endorse and apply the principles, the CMAT community will grow and mature. I sincerely hope that further changes and improvements will be made to the model, perhaps by others if not by myself.

THREE LEVELS OF APPLICATION

You may choose to apply the contents of this book in one of three ways. Each level goes deeper than the previous one, with increasing commitment and effort required than the previous one, but also with greater returns and rewards.

Level 1: *Your Own Ministry and Organisation*

Level 1 involves applying these principles to your own ministry practice. You may change some of the ways you approach the churches or agencies that you work with. You could share this within your own circles of influence—your boards and partners. Perhaps you could give a copy of this book to a missions partner and discuss what you thought about each partnership values. All of these examples relate to applying the CMAT principles to your current ministry and partnerships.

In addition to sharing principles with other leaders in your organisation, writing even a small portion of the material in this book into your own organisation's policy will be greatly beneficial on two levels. First, the process of inserting into organisational policy will ensure that key leaders discuss the concepts being introduced. In a church, key leaders may include elders, while in a missions agency, they would include board or council members. These people may not be directly involved in church-agency partnerships, but their support and understanding for future decisions is crucial. Second, any concepts introduced into policy have the potential to positively impact the next generation of leaders that come after you. For these two reasons, one of the simplest and most effective portions to insert into policy is the four partnership values of *REMCAP*. Churches and missions agencies may already have a section on their policy about partnership, but now there is potential for both to have the same values written into policy. In Chapter 5, the section on CMAT values provides four paragraphs, one for each value, which has been designed to be broad enough to insert into organisational policy. With this, an organisation can write, "Regarding partnerships with missions agencies/local churches, we adopt the following partnership values."

The authors and original CMAT group would be so pleased to hear if this material has been of help to you in this matter. If organisations you are partnering with start expressing interest in what you are doing, then you may also consider the next level of application.

Level 2: Your Own CMAT Group

Level 2 application would be to start your own CMAT group, thus becoming a part of the CMAT community. Like the participants of the first pilot CMAT group, you would enter a process of strengthening your partnership in community. In this case, you are interacting with not only one partner but multiple partners in a small group. Truly, 2+2 is greater than 4 in this scenario, because the mutual learning from the experiences of a wider group and growth through community processing of case studies are extremely powerful. This chapter will further describe the process and structures required for this. While changing the way you do things always requires some effort, the CMAT approach may not take more actual time, because you are meeting the several church or agency leaders that you need to meet anyway, but you are doing it at a scheduled time in a small CMAT group.

Level 3: Your Contribution to a Body of Knowledge

Level 3 is similar to a Level 2 CMAT group, except for the additional discipline of becoming part of an ongoing research process. This involves your group documenting your case studies and sharing your conclusions with others in the wider CMAT community, much like we have done in the practical chapters of Part 2 of this book. Level 3 means that you become part of an ongoing research process that would grow the body of data on church-agency partnership for others. In particular, we hope that others will write additional chapters on church and missions agency partnerships for issues we have not yet covered in this first book, or go deeper with increased specifics on topics that we have covered here more broadly. This possibility will also be discussed later in this chapter.

HOW TO START A CMAT GROUP

If you are choosing to apply the material in this book at Level 2 or Level 3, you will be starting your own CMAT group. Here are some handles on how to begin this group and what to do during your meetings.

Invite Friends and Existing Partners

Consider which members would be a good mix of leaders in this CMAT group. Invite friends whom you know already believe in church-agency partnerships and who are open to better practices. Also invite existing partners with whom you are already working. Some of the people you invite may want to bring in another friend or partner, and that would work, as long as the group consists of an approximately equal number of people representing churches and missions agencies.

Thus, the group should already have a network of pre-existing relationships among the members, and it is upon this network that you are adding the partnership values and *REMCAP*. You are aiming to discuss significant missions leadership matters in an environment where personal relationships are marked by joyful fellowship and encouragement. Therefore, it helps that some pre-existing friendships form the backbone of the group.

A second reason for going through existing networks and personal friends is that everyone already has a full plate of responsibilities. No one wants to commit to another regular group meeting, but you are likely to say "yes" to a meeting if a friend says to you, "I found this helpful resource about church-agency partnerships. Are you available to hear more about it and give your input on some missions partnership issues?" All members would have heard of chronic tensions between the church and agency with many having experienced them first-hand, but they have not likely discussed them openly. Thus, having some pre-existing trust relationships will aid the environment for discussion, and the relevance and freshness of the conversation will further increase interest.

If you already have one or more church or agency partners with whom you try to meet regularly, you already know the importance of having good communication before any crisis or difficulty arises. The final reason for starting with your existing partner network is that you should be meeting regularly with them anyway, and the CMAT group provides a structured and scheduled opportunity to do this in a way that creates a learning environment and greatly strengthens your partnership. While a CMAT group requires planning ahead and scheduling time, it will also save time because you can meet multiple partners together and you will be able to better manage problems that arise in the future.

Share the CMAT Book

In order for people to commit time for the first CMAT meeting, they need to feel that the commitment will be a good use of their time.

This book will be extremely helpful at this point, because people you invite will see that you are basing the group on a model that has been tested and endorsed by other groups of church and agency leaders. In other words, you are not calling a group "just to talk" but to build on a credible model of what others have done before.

Attendees will likely not be able to read the entire book before the first meeting and that is acceptable. The book will be a companion throughout your CMAT period together, not only for the first session.

Ensure Purposeful Clarity

Most leaders already have too many meetings that fill our lives, so your potential participants will only voluntarily commit to another one if they have a clear sense of purpose. Establish this by saying it, then repeating it, at your first few meetings.

We have found it helpful to write out a definition of who we are and the purpose of our meeting. We encapsulated this in a single paragraph that is printed in Chapter 5, "Who is CMAT". We share this description of ourselves with others so that like-minded missions leaders would know the culture of our group and join if they are led by the Spirit. Especially at our first few meetings, we would read it aloud together to remind ourselves who we are and why we meet.

> We, Churches and Missions Agencies Together, are a working group of missions leaders of churches and missions organisations in Singapore who expectantly recognise that partnerships between local churches and missions agencies have immense potential to advance world evangelisation. We are committed to

church-agency partnerships that reflect the image of Trinitarian relationships, incubate effective missions practice and nurture optimal missionary care. At the same time, we admit that the effective practice of such inter-organisational relationships is, unfortunately, rare. We know that our own partnership practice falls short, thus we seek to learn and work together within an environment of relational trust and transparency.

Notice that the purpose of the group is specific enough to form a cohesive group identity: learning and working together on our church-agency partnerships. Yet it is not so specific as to state how we will do this, how long we will commit to, or whether the working group will generate any tangible products. These aspects come later.

Time and Commitment

As the leader starting your CMAT group, your potential members will wonder how much time you are asking of them, for how long and what you will be doing in this period. We suggest that you set a fixed period of time to meet. We found that meeting for one full day, once every three months, for one year was an excellent place to begin. At the end of the year, celebrate the progress you have made and close the group joyfully, unless members feel that the work is not yet done and they would like to continue for an additional period of time.

The first CMAT group met for one year, and though we could have joyfully ended then, we continued to meet for a second year because we found it rewarding and we set ourselves the goal of writing this book together. Your goal at the end of one year will definitely include strengthened partnerships, mutual learning of partnership practice, and principles that are agreed upon within the group. These are all products of a CMAT meeting conducted at Level 2 of application.

With the additional commitment of documenting your discussions and working with the original CMAT authors, you yourselves could not only learn but also rise to Level 3 application. At this level, you help others by depositing your conclusions into a shared body of knowledge on church-agency partnerships. You could make a valuable contribution even within one year of meeting if your group agrees to write just one topic, forming one chapter in a future *Churches and Missions Agencies Together* volume. Such a goal would indeed be purposeful and well worth meeting once every three months for a year!

The remainder of this chapter will describe the elements that make up a CMAT group and the process for how this can be achieved.

ELEMENTS OF A CMAT GROUP

A working group of senior church and agency leaders is quite different from a typical small group gathering in a church and also unlike staff meetings that we are normally accustomed to. We have found the following key elements helpful as we progressed in our time as missions leaders over the course of the two years.

Food and Fellowship

Like many cultures, food is an important part of our fellowship in Singapore. Therefore, we intentionally begin our CMAT meetings with breakfast together. This sets the tone for our value of joyful fellowship and encouragement, and prioritises personal relationships in our meetings.

One of the things I explain is that, I try to build my personal relationships with missions partners to the point where I am looking forward to see them when we are about to meet. We should be friends with a common vision who do not get to meet up often due to our own responsibilities, so when we do see each other, we are glad and thankful for the other's valuable contribution to the friendship and the ministry. The CMAT gathering should be organised in such a way so as to nurture these types of relationships. When we meet quarterly, we look forward to the breakfast time that precedes our work discussions.

REMCAP and Partnership Values

In your first meeting, it will be necessary for someone to present *REMCAP* and the partnership values. Your group will then discuss their understanding of each of the partnership values and how they feel this can be applied to the leadership role in their organisation. If you need assistance in this, see the section titled "Starter Culture" below, where members of the original CMAT group will come help you get started and also teach some of the material.

Subsequent meetings will have less time devoted to discussing the material, as understanding would have grown and participants will all have similar understanding of the values and *REMCAP.*

Collaborative Learning

While some material is taught, the bulk of the learning and time should be collaborative in nature. Although the research and model frame and shape the group's view of church-agency partnerships, the decades of experience in the group fuel the group learning experience. As the leader of our original CMAT group, I constantly encouraged group participation and joint leadership in how each meeting was designed.

One way of doing this is having different people present topics in which they have expertise. This works very well when there is a topic relevant to the partnership issues at hand. In our group, one person presented an overview of the state of missions in Singapore, while another talked about critical issues in member care. We were careful to keep the topics always revolving around the focus of church-agency partnerships, as that was our group's distinctive. For example, when discussing member care, we did not drift into clinical aspects, but talked about how the church and missions agency contributed to member care and our respective roles.

Another method used to great effect was sticky-note discussions. This technique provides variety and stimulates creativity suited in a leadership environment. As the facilitator, I would pose one or more questions, and ask all participants to write their answers on a sticky-note, walk to a central discussion board where they would post it on the wall and remain standing. For example, the question could be, "What are some frustrations we observe between churches and missions agencies when partnering to send a missionary?"

As more people gathered and stood around the board, their change in posture and physical location in the room stimulated interaction. I sometimes clustered Post-It Notes topically so we could see patterns emerge as the group posted more notes. I would take a note, read it aloud then ask, "Who wrote that? Can you tell us more?" The group would stand and interact for long periods in this manner, discussing various issues. Often the questions were open-ended, designed to generate discussion. As the group trust level increased, more sensitive and difficult questions could be asked. At other times, for variety, the questions included, "Do you agree with this statement...", and participants stuck circles on a large Likert scale ranging from "strongly disagree" to "strongly agree". I obtained a sense of where the group was at on this issue and asked, "Who put this sticker here? Can you tell us why?"

Finally, an absolutely crucial means of collaborative learning was employing case studies. This is so important that it was the mainstay of our meetings and will be discussed at length in the next section.

THE MAINSTAY OF CASE STUDIES

The previous elements that comprised a CMAT meeting encourage collaborative learning, but the case study method we employed took this to a whole other level. From the very first CMAT meeting, we invited participants to come with a case study written for the group to explore, and we encourage you to do the same.

Writing a Case Study

Case studies are best written and presented by members of the group, thus ensuring active participation by all. Since members brought a variety of real-life experiences to the table, the discussion was extremely rich. We gave the following guidelines for writing and bringing a case study to each CMAT meeting.

1. The purpose of the case study is to explore application of the partnership values and *REMCAP* to actual church-agency partnership practice. The purpose is achieved when exploration culminates in good practice guidelines that are agreed upon, and ideally documented, by members of the CMAT group representing a range of churches and missions agencies.

2. The topic of the case study could be an actual incident or a composite of factual incidents and situations. The case study should not identify particular individuals, but may identify organisations within the CMAT working group when permission from the organisation's representative is granted. Discussing real situations, in the presence of representatives of those organisations, brings great depth and authenticity to the application of values and writing of good practice guidelines.[15]

3. The case study should be brief, comprising 100–250 words. This length includes two to four specific questions at the end of the case study that direct the ensuing discussion. The questions should highlight the specific topic at hand and draw out good church-agency partnership practice guidelines that the group seeks to agree upon.

Discussion and Documentation

The people with whom you are starting the group may not be accustomed to this type of group work, or they may think they already know it because they have discussed some form of case studies before. The important message to give them is that the case studies will follow a specific format and they are not pre-determined by any facilitator or course material. Instead, participants themselves are writing the case studies and the group will discuss them around a biblical and theological framework. Further, you are all not attending a seminar; you are a working group with an objective to reach agreed upon good practices on this case study. Your participants will find this challenging yet meaningful, because the generating of good practices by agreement of a group of church and agency leaders in transparent discussion is a valuable and distinctive characteristic of a CMAT group.

Some cases will be written from either a distinctly church perspective or a distinctively missions agency perspective, and this is perfectly acceptable. We find these perspectives bring an invigorating level of authenticity to the group, with even personal pain and frustration sometimes expressed by the church or agency leader presenting the case study. Such sharing encourages a deeper level of understanding by leaders on the other side of the church-agency partnership. Authenticity increased in an environment of joyful fellowship and encouragement.

Ask the person who wrote the case study to present it to the group by reading aloud and briefly answering any additional questions. He or she will then decide how to divide the CMAT group into smaller discussion groups to explore the questions. Sometimes, we mixed church and agency leaders together, other times we formed one "church group" and one "agency group" to see what different perspectives would arise. Each subgroup discusses for an allotted time, then presents their findings to the large group. Assign someone to document the findings and distribute a written summary to the group after the meeting. This tangible record of agreed upon good practice is a "small win" and a great motivator for the group that the time spent is a worthwhile investment, because not many groups are able to produce tangible products that benefit not only its members, but also others with whom the guidelines will be shared.

Research Publications

The "small win" of a written summary becomes a "big win" when it is written at a standard worthy of publication. If that written summary can be refined, the analysis explained and conclusions presented with clarity, then the case study can become the material for one chapter in the next volume of *Churches and Missions Agencies Together*.

Give your case study a descriptive title. You will find that some case studies elaborate on subjects already discussed in this book, while others venture into new areas. The first CMAT group wrote up 12 case studies and selected six of them to be the seeds from which our six chapters in Part 2 of this book would grow. We chose them because we felt they were foundational topics, but we know there are many more important topics to explore. For example, we had no case studies on Third-Culture Kid (TCK) issues, missional business ventures, or dealing with discipline or ministry failure. Many more areas remain ripe for exploration. As you write and discuss your case studies, you will gain clarity, and the original CMAT group is eager to work with you to share that newfound clarity with others. To illustrate what a written summary of one of our case studies looked like before being inserted into a chapter, see samples in *Appendix 1: Missionary Candidature Assessment and Concerns* and *Appendix 2: Direct-Sent Missionary Desires Sending Through Agency*.

As discussions proceed around additional case studies, I hope that the *REMCAP* values presented in this book will continue to be amended and improved by others, not only by myself. For example, the original research never uncovered TCK issues because it did not surface in the interviews. This does not mean it that it is an unimportant issue but rather because time for the interviews was limited. Future case studies could investigate how churches and agencies could best partner in the life and ministry of TCKs. Another CMAT group could write their conclusions and contribute to shared knowledge by working with us on a second joint publication.

CONCLUSION: STARTER CULTURE

I recently discovered the joys of making yoghurt at home. The silky, creamy texture of home-made yoghurt surpasses the store-bought variety and the taste is full yet less tart. If you mix just one teaspoon of yoghurt with live and active cultures into one litre of milk and wait for eight hours with the mixture at the right temperature, that one teaspoon of "starter culture" yoghurt magically turns the milk into delicious yoghurt. The ingredients of yoghurt are already in the milk—all that is needed are the right starter culture and the right environment.

You very likely have all that is needed to nurture your own CMAT group, yet having a starter culture helps to get the process going. Missions leaders who have participated in one CMAT group are the perfect starter for another group that is seeking help to form. When one group ends, having one church leader and one missions leader help to start another CMAT group with different church and agency leaders is ideal. They are that one teaspoon of starter culture for the next batch of CMAT discussion.

The original members of the first CMAT pilot working group offer our presence to others who wish to begin their own groups of CMAT. We have joyfully concluded our own meeting when we completed this book and now make ourselves available to other groups, hoping to continue our learning as we participate in church-agency partnership research by adding to this body of data on how we can better practise our partnerships.

Therefore, alongside our testimony in this book, we offer our participation to help your CMAT group begin. This could include some teaching, being a working part of the group that meets for a year, or collaborating on publishing a second volume of this book with more chapters written on partnership topics based on case studies that you generate. May God guide us to grow a culture among church and missions agency leaders that is more joyful in relationship and effective in partnership, because we bring to realisation the divine blueprint of truly being churches and missions agencies together.

APPENDIX 1

Ivan Liew

SAMPLE CASE STUDIES:
Missionary Candidate Assessment & Concerns

Henry's contract with his church as a full-time ministry staff was ending. He and his wife felt called to serve in the mission field. He had prior working experience with a missions organisation, and began to enquire with a missions agency. The agency saw ministry possibilities for Henry and his wife, and requested to meet with their missions pastor and elder. At that meeting, the church leaders gave feedback on Henry's strengths and weaknesses, and asked about what roles Henry and his wife would play. They commented that Henry would need a lot of "hand-holding" if he were given a role requiring him to take initiative. He would do well if he were only assigned tasks to do. Further, they did not see his passion for missions. Finally, the church had its own screening procedure for members interested in missions and they felt the church might not be behind Henry if he were to go through with the church's process.

The missions agency would like the church's approval for Henry and his wife to apply with them. The church leaders wanted Henry to be processed internally by the church before they gave their response to the agency. The church leaders did not have whole-hearted support for him to join the agency. Therefore, they expressed their reservations, saying they would leave it to the agency leaders to form their own opinion and come to their own decision.

1. Since there is reservation on the part of the church to fully support Henry and his wife's application with the missions agency, should the agency still proceed with the application seeing that Henry felt this is what the Lord would have for them in their next ministry phase? Why or why not?

2. Should the missions agency seek to find out from Henry his "side of the story" with regards to the concerns raised by his church leaders? Why or why not? How will this affect the potential partnership relationship between the church and the missions agency?

3. How could the church, agency and missionary communicate and work better together in a mobilisation scenario such as this?

Group Analysis

The weakest link in this scenario is the relationship between Henry and his church leaders. Unfortunately, it appears that Henry is not aware of the depth of his church leaders' concerns. Perhaps he had not talked sufficiently with his missions pastor about his interest, or even if he had, their evaluation of his suitability to be sent by the church was either not communicated or not heard.

At this stage, the agency should not proceed with Henry's application. Based on CMAT values, we must esteem one another's contributions and opinions. If the agency were to go ahead immediately based on their need and Henry's willingness, they would not be affirming the biblical centrality of the church.

The church said, "We will make our decision, you make yours."

Unfortunately, this statement reflects independent decision-making rather than healthy interdependence in the partnership. When the church has reservations, these must be addressed with the missionary directly. It would be even better to address them together with the missions agency, as is possible in Henry's case.

Practically, it is often the church leaders who know the candidate better, over a longer period of time, and in the broader picture of their family and personal lives, and not only their ministry. In Henry's case, the church also knew him as a ministry staff, so the missions agency should pay close heed to the church's reservations even if they do not share the same concerns.

While the missions agency should not proceed immediately with the application, the agency leaders would do well to find out how they can help Henry discern his calling, regardless of whether he is aware of his church leader's concerns, and advise him on how he can address them. A church tends to look for qualities of leadership, initiative, independence and high capacity when screening missionaries. Such qualities are deemed highly valuable, and for some churches even a requirement, even though certain positions that the missions agency has in mind may not necessitate such abilities. As a third party, the agency can advise and counsel Henry on aspects that his leaders want to see evidenced, and weaknesses of which he may need to be aware. If the agency's intended ministry role does not require some of these qualities, further discussion with the church may alleviate some of the church leaders' reservations. The agency may also have access to specialist resources, screenings and psychological profiles that would help all leaders make better informed decisions.

Concerns that the church-agency relationship may be negatively impacted need not arise if communication about Henry's evaluation is kept open, and three-way sharing between the church, agency and missionary candidate is conducted. *REMCAP* recommends that church-agency communication begin early, at the stage of missionary candidature and selection; however, this is often lacking. More often than not, churches make their own selection independently without involving the agency. In all cases, but especially when concerns arise such as in Henry's example, greater communication with the missions agency would be helpful for all parties involved, especially the missionary candidate.

SAMPLE CASE STUDY:
Direct-Sent Missionary Desires Sending Through Agency

With the blessing of their church, Anthony and Mary left their jobs, equipped themselves with night classes at a bible college, and were direct-sent by their local church to a small city in China. The first year was focused on improving their Mandarin language, study and connecting with their local neighbours. They began to feel very much alone in their ministry. The home church kept in contact, but the difficult reality of being far away set in. At the time, they met other missionaries in their city from various missions agencies. These missionaries became a source of encouragement and fellowship for Anthony and Mary.

As they began their second year in China, they felt that field ministry was more challenging than they had first anticipated. They shared with their sending church about their desire to work and serve through a missions agency in that same field. To ensure that they were able to stay long term and be effective on the field, they desired member care, supervision, accountability, and team members with whom to discuss and consult.

1. How can a missionary best communicate their desires and needs to their direct-sending church if they are in a similar situation?

2. How can a church and agency dialogue to possibly convert a direct-sending situation into a church-agency sending partnership?

3. What difficulties and challenges would the church and missions agency mutually face in light of the background, and how can these be mitigated?

Group Analysis

A shift in sending coverage is a tremendous change that the missionary is seeking, so homework and preparation before making this request is crucial. The missionary must have a thorough understanding of their church's policies regarding missionary sending, and the policies surrounding them being direct-sent to the field. The rationale and background of the church choosing to direct-send must first be thoroughly understood by the missionary before requesting a change. For example, a church may have had successful direct-sending experience to one mission field previously, but the situation may have been vastly different from the current one being faced. Or church leaders may have had a negative experience with a missions agency, leading them to choose direct-sending, in which case understanding this negative experience would be crucial. Sometimes, churches may simply not be exposed to missions agencies, and the missionary may need to initiate the relationship between his church and the missions agency leadership.

One approach is to encourage a field visit of church leaders, and to share with them the difficulty of ministry and the contextual challenges faced. Such challenges are best shared in the midst of reality of field ministry, rather than in the church boardroom during a home visit. On the field, church leaders could meet other missionaries who are potential partners, hear about ministry of the missions agency team on the field, and thus gain personal knowledge about the people that the missionary wishes to partner with. Alignment of vision and ministry philosophy between the church and agency is a key factor that the church leader must see during a field visit.

The missionary must be wise in planning such a field visit for his church leaders. Certain field realities can't be fully reproduced for a leader visiting on a short trip. Low budget constraints, the feeling of isolation and loneliness, and the challenge of daily life with limited language are not experienced by a church leader with a generous budget who stays for five days in a hotel. Balanced choices must be made. Sometimes, a missionary plans a trip for his church leaders, carefully ensuring that everything is smooth and comfortable for them, which results in them thinking, "The field is not that difficult. Why is my missionary having such a difficult time?"

Communication with church leaders, whether on the field or at home, must demonstrate why ministry is more effective when working with the missions agency. A direct-sending church must be convinced that the missions agency is adding value to the missionary endeavour. They are already convicted about biblical centrality of the church in missions, so by comprehending what the missions agency brings to the partnership, they can equally value the missions agency and consider a partnership. The missionary should aim to help the church understand why direct-sending is not helping him in this scenario. *REMCAP* can serve as a framework for such sharing, showing that the church is a critically necessary support, but that a different type of support is needed on the field, which best comes from a missions agency with a strong field presence.

A church-agency-missionary dialogue that is based on biblical values and a partnership framework is more likely to be fruitful. Affirming a direct-sending church's biblical role and its effort and responsibility in missions is an excellent launching point to help church leaders understand a missions agency's potential contribution and consider a sending partnership. If a church is willing to consider this, the missions agency must be mindful of the perceived risk that the church must deal with. For example, the church must release some amount of field supervision, control and strategy. Managing this trepidation and risk can be done with shared values, *REMCAP*, and guidelines for good practice. Clarifying roles and responsibilities during the partnership discussion would help to facilitate good communication and building of trust, which would overcome any perceived risk.

APPENDIX 2

RECOMMENDED READING

Chapter 1: Churches and Missions Agencies in Singapore

Metcalf, Sam, and Alan Hirsch. *Beyond the Local Church: How Apostolic Movements Can Change the World*. Downers Grove: IVP Books, 2015. Print.

Stiles, Mack. "Nine Marks of a Healthy Parachurch Ministry." *Church and Parachurch: Friends or Foes?*. Ed. Jonathan Leeman and Bobby Jamieson. 9Marks, 2011. Print.

Tan, Kang San. "Who Is in the Driver's Seat?" *Understanding Asian Mission Movements: Proceedings of the Asian Mission Consultation 2008-2010*. Gloucester, UK: Wide Margin, 2010. Print.

White, Jerry. *The Church and the Parachurch: An Uneasy Marriage*. Portland, OR: Multnomah Press, 1983. Print.

Chapter 2: Biblical, Theological & Historical Foundations

Hammett, John S. "How Church and Parachurch Should Relate : Arguments for a Servant-Partnership Model." *Missiology* 28.2 (2000): 199–207. Print.

---. "Church and Parachurch as Two Equal Structures: A Historical and Theological Critique." *Evangelical Theological Society* (1998): 1–15. Print.

Ross, Cathy. "The Theology of Partnership." International Bulletin of Missionary Research 34.3 (2010): 145–148. Print.

Tennent, Timothy. Invitation to World Missions: A Trinitarian Missiology for the Twenty-First Century. Kregel Academic, 2010. Print.

Winter, R. D. "The Two Structures of God's Redemptive Mission." *Missiology* 2.1 (1974): 121–139. Print.

Chapter 3: *A Research Study on Church-Agency Partnerships*

Behar, Lee. "Reflection on a Missions Partnership." *Evangelical Missions Quarterly* (2008): n. pag. Web. 26 Oct. 2009.

Beirn, Steve. "Building the Church/Agency Relationship." *Evangelical Missions Quarterly* n. pag. Web. 12 Oct. 2010.

Wuthnow, Robert. *Boundless Faith: The Global Outreach of American Churches*. 1st ed. University of California Press, 2010. Print.

Chapter 4: *The Relational Model of Church-Agency Partnerships*

Beirn, Steve. *Well Sent: Reimagining the Church's Missionary-Sending Process*. CLC Publications, 2015. Print.

Borthwick, P. "What Local Churches Are Saying to Mission Agencies." *Evangelical Missions Quarterly* 35.3 (1999): 324–33. Print.

Knell, Bryan. *The Heart of Church and Mission*. Nürnberg: VTR Publications, 2015. Print.

Metcalf, Samuel F. "When Local Churches Act Like Agencies." *Evangelical Missions Quarterly* (1993): n. pag. Web. 12 Oct. 2010.

Price, Keith. "Cooperating in World Evangelization: A Handbook on Church/Para-

Church Relationships." Lausanne Movement. N.p., 1 Mar. 1983. Web. 26 Sept. 2015.

Sharp, Larry. "What an Agency Leader Would Say to Local Churches." *Evangelical Missions Quarterly* 36.1 (2000): 78–83. Print.

Chapter 7: *Communication & Commitment*

Hughes, R. Kent, and Barbara Hughes. *Liberating Ministry from the Success Syndrome.* Crossway Books, 2008. Print.

Seamands, Stephen. Ministry in the Image of God: The Trinitarian Shape of Christian Service. IVP Books, 2005. Print.

Willard, Dallas. Living in Christ's Presence: Final Words on Heaven and the Kingdom of God. InterVarsity Press, 2014. Print.

Chapter 8: *Missionary Candidature & Preparation*

Bacon, Daniel W. Equipping for Missions: A Guide to Making Career Decisions. OMF International, 1992. Print.

Lane, Denis. *Tuning God's New Instruments*. World Evangelical Fellowship, 1990. Print.

Chapter 10: *Conflict*

Elmer, Duane. Cross-Cultural Conflict: Building Relationships for Effective Ministry. InterVarsity Press, 1993. Print.

---. Cross-Cultural Servanthood: Serving the World in Christlike Humility. InterVarsity Press, 2009. Print.

Gardner, Laura Mae. Healthy, Resilient, & Effective in Cross-Cultural Ministry. Condeo Press, 2016. Print.

"Sharpening Your Interpersonal Skills." *International Training Partners, Web. www. relationshipskills.com.*

Chapter 11: Crisis Management

Floyd, Scott. *Crisis Counseling: A Guide for Pastors and Professionals.* Grand Rapids, MI: Kregel Academic & Professional, 2008. Print.

Schaefer, Charles A. *Trauma and Resilience: A Handbook.* Ed. Frauke C. Schaefer. Condeo Press, 2016. Print.

Singapore government agencies relevant in times of crises:

Ministry of Health. http://www.moh.gov.sg/

"Travel Notices/Advisories." *Ministry of Foreign Affairs.* http://www.mfa.gov.sg/

"When Death Occurs Overseas." *National Environment Agency.* http://www.nea.gov.sg/

World and local news helpful in times of crises:

BBC News, UK. http://news.bbc.co.uk

Channel NewsAsia, Singapore. http://www.channelnewsasia.com/*CNN, USA.* http://www.cnn.com/world

"Global Display of Terrorism and Other Suspicious Events" *Global Incident Map.* http://www.globalincidentmap.com

NOTES

1. See "Lee Kuan Yew's Singapore: An astonishing record." *The Economist.* 22 Mar 2015. Web. 7 Sep 2016.

2. The Joshua Project reports that 6,686 of the 16,508 people groups worldwide were still considered "unreached." See "Global Statistics." Joshua Project. Web. 7 Sep 2016. www.joshuaproject.net/global_statistics.

3. The much quoted figures are from the Gordon-Cornwall Theological Seminary 2010 Statistics which showed that Singapore was one of the highest sending nations of missionaries per million (m.p.m.) church members. This is different from a separate list for absolute numbers of missionaries sent. Singapore emerged an impressive seventh on the list with 815 m.p.m. church members. It was only preceded by Palestine (3,401 m.p.m.), Ireland (2,131 m.p.m.), Malta (1,994 m.p.m.), Samoa (1,802 m.p.m.) and South Korea (1,014 m.p.m.).

4. The Scope of Missions: Report for SCGM National Missions Survey 2014. Singapore Centre for Global Mission. 2014.

5. Echoing a statement by then Prime Minister Goh Chok Tong in his 2001 National Day speech and subsequently picked up by some church movements. Goh Chock Tong. "National Day Rally Address" *National Archives of Singapore.* 19 Aug 2001. Web. 8 Sep 2016.

6. Woodlands Evangelical Free Church (Singapore) is an actual local church where the original research on church-agency partnerships originated. The names of churches and missions agencies in Part 2 of this book are fictitious.

7. Other concepts surrounding partnerships were discussed by some agency directors, but these were not as cohesively connected with other concepts

as the five key ingredients already mentioned. Strategy, policies and accountability were some of these important elements raised, but they did not feature as centrally when discussing the understanding and practice of church-agency partnerships. Chapter 6 deals with how strategy differs from vision and ministry philosophy.

8. Further details on how these partnership values were derived can be found in Chapter 2.

9. In our initial documents we defined ourselves as a "pilot working group" to indicate that as the first CMAT group, we aimed for a depth of interaction and relationship that we felt was only possible by remaining as a small group. Our desire, however, was never to be exclusive, but to share the values and principles we are developing with others. The formation and collaboration of additional groups, with more churches and missions agencies involved, will further strengthen the model and jointly developed good practice guidelines.

10. *Perichoresis* is a special term used to describe the Trinitarian relationship. More than a relationship between three separate individuals, it points to the inter-penetration of the three persons in the Godhead, being simultaneously three distinct persons yet one God.

11. In order to maximise clarity and present the most updated model, the previous chapters in this book describe *REMCAP* after improvements were made.

12. Our group also took up the additional task of documenting each case study and writing a summary for dissemination and agreement by all participants. This extra effort was taken because we aimed to share the results with others though this book.

13. See "Trinitarian Basis for Partnership" in Chapter 2.

14. A corollary can be seen with the metaphor of remaining in the vine as Christ explains in John 15. When we commit to one another in Christ, we

help one another remain in the vine of Jesus. Only in this manner shall we bear fruit that lasts.

15. While the original CMAT group discussed our own struggles and our organisations, we did not share real names of people or partnering organisations with other members of CMAT. Case studies that are written in this book had further details changed so that they would be unrecognisable.

BIBLIOGRAPHY

Barrett, David B. et al. *World Christian Trends, AD 30-AD 2200: Interpreting the Annual Christian Megacensus*. Pasadena, CA: William Carey Library, 2001. Print.

Beirn, Steve. *Well Sent: Reimagining the Church's Missionary-Sending Process*. CLC Publications, 2015. Print.

Bonk, Jonathan J. "What About Partnership?" *International Bulletin of Missionary Research* 34.3 (2010): 129–130. Print.

Carey, William. *An Enquiry into the Obligations of Christians to Use Means for the Conversion of the Heathens*. Gloucester, UK: Dodo Press, 2007. Print.

Cunningham, David S. *These Three Are One: The Practice of Trinitarian Theology*. Hoboken, NJ: Wiley-Blackwell, 1998. Print.

Das, T. K., and Bing-Sheng Teng. "Trust, Control, and Risk in Strategic Alliances: An Integrated Framework." *Organisation Studies* 22.2 (2001): 251–283. *EBSCOhost*. Web.

Eckman, James P. *Exploring Church History*. Wheaton, IL: Crossway Books, 2002. Print.

Elmer, Duane. *Cross-Cultural Servanthood: Serving the World in Christlike Humility*. 2.6.2006 edition. Downers Grove, Ill: IVP Books, 2006. Print.

Fung, P. "Missions Asia: Practical Models in Mission Partnership." *Understanding Asian Mission Movements: Proceedings of the Asian Mission Consultation 2008-2010*. Gloucester, UK: Wide Margin, 2010. Print.

Goh, Daniel PS. "State and Social Christianity in Post-Colonial Singapore." *Sojourn: Journal of Social Issues in Southeast Asia* 25.1 (2010): 54–89. Print.

Hammett, John S. "How Church and Parachurch Should Relate : Arguments for a Servant-Partnership Model." *Missiology* 28.2 (2000): 199–207. Print.

Hutton, J.E. *A History of the Moravian Church*. Charleston, SC: BiblioBazaar, 2007. Print.

Jenkins, Philip. *The Next Christendom: The Coming of Global Christianity*. Oxford University Press, 2007. Print.

Knell, Bryan. *The Heart of Church and Mission*. Nürnberg: VTR Publications, 2015. Print.

Latourette, Kenneth Scott. *A History of the Expansion of Christianity (Vol. 4): The Great Century—Europe and the United States*. Grand Rapids, MI: Zondervan, 1974. Print.

Lausanne Committee for World Evangelization. "Cooperating in World Evangelization: A Handbook on Church/Para-Church Relationships." N.p., 1983. n. pag. Print.

Metcalf, Sam, and Alan Hirsch. *Beyond the Local Church: How Apostolic Movements Can Change the World*. Downers Grove: IVP Books, 2015. Print.

Pierson, Paul E. "Local Churches in Mission: What's Behind the Impatience with Traditional Mission Agencies?" *International Bulletin of Missionary Research* 22.4 (1998): 146. *EBSCOhost*. Web.

Priest, Robert J., Douglas Wilson, and Adelle Johnson. "U.S. Megachurches and New Patterns of Global Mission." *International Bulletin of Missionary Research* 34.2 (2010): 97–102. Print.

Ross, Cathy. "The Theology of Partnership." *International Bulletin of Missionary Research* 34.3 (2010): 145–148. Print.

Schaff, Philip. *History of the Christian Church*. Charles Scribner's Sons, 1908. Print.

Schattschneider, D. A. "William Carey, Modern Missions, and the Moravian Influence." *International Bulletin of Missionary Research* 22 (1998): 8–12. Print.

Sharp, Larry. "What an Agency Leader Would Say to Local Churches." *Evangelical Missions Quarterly* 36.1 (2000): 78–83. Print.

Shaw, Mark. *Doing Theology with Huck & Jim: Parables for Understanding Doctrine*. Eugene, OR: Wipf & Stock Publishers, 2004. Print.

Tan, Kang San. "Who Is in the Driver's Seat?" *Understanding Asian Mission Movements: Proceedings of the Asian Mission Consultation 2008-2010*. Gloucester, UK: Wide Margin, 2010. Print.

Tennent, Timothy. *Invitation to World Missions: A Trinitarian Missiology for the Twenty-First Century*. Kregel Academic, 2010. Print.

Walker, Williston. *A History of the Christian Church*. General Books LLC, 2010. Print.

White, Jerry. *The Church and the Parachurch: An Uneasy Marriage*. Portland, OR: Multnomah Press, 1983. Print.

Winter, R. D. "The Two Structures of God's Redemptive Mission." *Missiology* 2.1 (1974): 121–139. Print.

Winter, Ralph D. *Frontiers in Mission: Discovering and Surmounting Barriers to the Missio Dei*. Pasadena, CA: William Carey International University Press, 2005. Print.

Wuthnow, Robert. *Boundless Faith: The Global Outreach of American Churches*. 1st ed. University of California Press, 2010. Print.

Made in the USA
Columbia, SC
08 October 2023

24098466R00148